Reuben Farley

Reuben Farley

The Man Of West Bromwich

Pauline Lawley and Anne Wilkins

BREWIN BOOKS

We dedicate this book to
Thomas William Dashwood Farley,
the great grandson of Reuben Farley
with our thanks for his time
and encouragement.

BREWIN BOOKS
56 Alcester Road,
Studley,
Warwickshire,
B80 7LG
www.brewinbooks.com

Published by Brewin Books 2015

A CIP catalogue record for this book is available from the
British Library.

ISBN: 978-1-85858-545-1

Printed and bound in Great Britain by
Bell & Bain Ltd.

"If Bradford had its Titus Salt,

Manchester had its John Bright,

Birmingham had its Joseph Chamberlain,

then West Bromwich was fortunate

to have Reuben Farley"

Quote from Carl Chinn
"From Little Acorns Grow"

ACKNOWLEDGEMENTS

There are a number of people to whom we must express our grateful thanks for their assistance in helping us to compile this book.

Carl Chinn and Rick Trainor for allowing us to use their respective articles on Reuben Farley.

The staff at Sandwell Community and History Archive Services for their help in our research using old newspaper articles and photographs.

Jonathan and Tom Farley for sharing their family genealogy research and photographs.

Robin Pearson for his support and guidance in his role as editor.

Bob, of Bob Everitt Design, for his expertise with many of the photographs and images.

Lynne Pearce for her permission to include her poem on the Oak House

Moreen Wilkes for her time from the start of the project.

Last but not least the West Bromwich Local History Society for their support in the very important task of getting the book published.

INTRODUCTION
by Robin Pearson

I T IS difficult to imagine in these days of career politicians on expenses and allowances that someone could combine the running of successful business enterprises with the promotion and provision of everyday services for fellow citizens. Such was the achievement of Reuben Farley who more than a hundred years after his death is remembered at every turn in West Bromwich by something named after him, or whose name appears on plaques and foundation stones throughout the town.

At the time of his birth West Bromwich had already started to expand from a scattered village community into a fast growing town – it was one of two places in England where the population multiplied six times within a few decades. What passed for civil administration in those days was ill-equipped to cope. Somehow what was called the Vestry Meeting tried to maintain law and order with parish constables and look after roads with Highway Surveyors. Basic services such as proper sanitation were non-existent until Town Improvement Commissioners were appointed in the 1850s.

Farley would join the Commissioners, becoming chairman in 1872 following on from the previous decade when he and his brother-in-law had purchased the Summit Foundry to form the successful company of Taylor & Farley. He applied his business acumen to his new local government role to provide the town with what it lacked in municipal buildings, mostly on a not too grand a scale so as to appease any likely criticism.

Eventually, when the town received borough status in 1882, he was the only man for the mayoralty – a reward, which Richard Trainor described, for being 'a classic example of the many Victorian businessmen who were active and influential leaders in the public affairs of industrial towns'.

In the West Midlands these businessmen lived close to their roots and, more importantly, their factories. Various families had a sustained and marked influence on their communities – the Chances in Smethwick, the Chamberlains in Birmingham, the Manders in Wolverhampton, and the Owens in Darlaston. In West Bromwich there were families such as Bagnall, Kenrick, and Salter, who, like the early Cadburys, improved the lot of their own workers and their families first and foremost but not the wider community as in the case of the first-mentioned dynasties.

Reuben Farley fulfilled a one generation role somewhat like contemporaries in Bilston, Brownhills, Dudley and Netherton. Reuben's children were young when he died, so there was no sense of family continuity in the local community as in the case of the Chance or Chamberlain families.

What makes Reuben Farley so special is what he did during his lifetime and how those things live on today. From his writings it can be seen that he could pick an idea from someone else's work and apply it in West Bromwich. He could persuade people to his way of thinking, as in his friendship with the Earl of Dartmouth, but that would have unforeseen consequences with the acquisition of Dartmouth Park. It led to pleas for open spaces from other districts of the town. Sometimes the solution for another park lay in Farley putting his own money into the enterprise such as at Greets Green.

Reuben Farley never did anything for the short term. He showed amazing capacity for longevity in every role he undertook, such as being on the hospital board for thirty years. He was elected President of the West Bromwich Building Society in 1864 and thirty-three years later, at the time of Queen Victoria's Diamond Jubilee, he was still holding that office. As various services and organisations were set up for the expanding population of West Bromwich, often someone else held the job of chairman at first and then Farley was elected as their replacement. When it came to being mayor, Farley was the first choice as first citizen, and again, and again. When he finally stepped down, he became deputy mayor – something his immediate successors as mayor did not do. It is not like today when a councillor often becomes the deputy before holding the top job, and certainly not deputy after their tenure as mayor. Was it that Farley could not give up, or that his fellow council members wanted to keep him near the top? Whatever it was, his energy seemed boundless and amid all his municipal/philanthropic work he was still the successful businessman.

One of the things that come over in his writings is his acknowledgement of the work of others, and how they helped him to achieve improvements for West Bromwich and its people. He would write on the function of the Institute that 'it would not be fair to leave out the names' of those who 'rendered most valuable assistance'. It was not just people of his own social status that he thanked but he gave 'credit' to school managers and teachers, and expressed 'confidence in the skill and ability' of medical staff, as well as acknowledging the 'marked ability' of the Clerk to the Town Improvement Commissioners in preparing their case in the gas dispute with Birmingham. And four years later he says 'I had the pleasure of turning on the gas in the presence of my colleagues'.

As an industrialist Farley could be 'stern' and unfriendly to 'grandmotherly legislation' and critical of union leaders, according to Richard Trainor. On the other hand, he could be moved to do something when he saw the 'dull, heavy and sullen appearance of the children in the workhouse'. Not only could he negotiate with the Earl of Dartmouth for land that would become Dartmouth Park but later he could find time on a Sunday to walk through it in the company of the Park Keeper.

In an article published in 2007 the Black Country historian Dr Trevor Raybould alluded to the local nobility's enlightened attitude to their employees, and their 'role of social benefactors in wider society'. As the old order of parish and manorial governance was superseded by town and borough status, those who ran these new administrations embraced the 'civic gospel' described by Professor Carl Chinn. On the far northerly edge of the Black Country there was someone who epitomised that gospel by being a church warden, a civic leader, and successful businessman. His name was William Roberts of Brownhills.

Both Roberts and Farley were born within a year of each other and both lived into their seventies.

As Brownhills developed out of the older Ogley Hey it needed, like West Bromwich, an improved form of local administration as it progressed from District Board to Urban District Council. Roberts was chairman of both, in the same way that Farley went from Town Improvement Commissioner to mayor. Again like Farley, Roberts gave land to the community and even presented the UDC with a brand new fire engine.

Another similarity between the two men was how they almost predicted their end. At one banquet Farley said 'As a native of West Bromwich I have striven, and should still strive, to the end of my days, to do what I can towards the advancement of the town'. In the week before his death he had attended a meeting. Roberts had 'even apologised in advance for his impending death and the trouble it would cause' as regards council duties. The subsequent funerals would see many mourners, and thousands on the streets paying their respects.

Again as Carl Chinn puts it in his piece on *Black Country People*, the names of the region's industrialists-cum-philanthropists still 'resonate' in the localities where they 'believed intensely in owing a duty'.

Pauline Lawley and Anne Wilkins have gathered together material from various sources – some items for the first time brought to the attention of a wider audience, otherwise going unnoticed in various documents. They have also assembled extracts from past writers such as newspaper columnist William Ellery Jephcott together with published pieces from present day historians Carl Chinn and Richard Trainor. The writers of this book have interwoven all these contributions with their own research and words to pay a worthy tribute to the man who made West Bromwich.

NOTES on AUTHORS
and CONTRIBUTORS

Pauline Anne Lawley is the secretary of the West Bromwich Local History Society and is on the committee of the Friends of Dartmouth Park. West Bromwich born Pauline organises the annual local Trafalgar Dinner which honours the memories of local sailors such as Captain James Eaton.

Anne Wilkins is also West Bromwich born. She is a retired teacher who has served on the committees of various friends groups such as for West Bromwich Library, the Oak House, and Sandwell Archives. In 2004 she won a Library Services Trust award for her book, *West Bromwich Town Hall*.

J.W.A. Aston (CHAPTER TWO) A West Bromwich resident who wrote and published in the 1960s *The Story of West Bromwich*.

Lavinia Benbow (CHAPTER TWO) was the West Bromwich author of two novels – *The Old Oak House: a tale of the seventeenth century* 1899 and *The Mystic Chain* 1929.

Carl Chinn (CHAPTER ONE) is a well known Midlands media personality who has done so much particularly through his local radio shows to popularise local heritage. A professor of community history at Birmingham University he has had many books and articles published with an emphasis on the Black Country. He has taken a keen interest in promoting West Bromwich history and has recently become President of the West Bromwich Local History Society.

Jonathan Farley (CHAPTER ELEVEN) is the great-great-grandson of John Farley, an older brother of Reuben Farley. He researched, with input from other family members, not only their ancestry back to the mid-eighteenth century but has traced the descendants of Reuben's siblings.

William Ellery Jephcott (CHAPTERS TWO, THREE, SEVEN and TEN) wrote between 1943 and 1946 a series of weekly newspaper articles on West Bromwich local history. These have become a valuable record of local buildings and streets many of which survived into the 1950s but were lost in the redevelopments of the 1960s and the 1970s and even up to today. He had books published on West Bromwich Albion and local industry – in particular *The House of Izons: the History of a Pioneer Firm of Ironfounders.*

Frederick B. Ludlow (CHAPTER NINE) was the editor of *County Biographies, 1901 (Staffordshire)* containing an obituary of Reuben Farley. He was also the author of *Black Country Tales and Sketches.*

Lynne Pearce (CHAPTER SEVEN) is a West Bromwich poet now living in Shropshire. Her poem, *Oak House*, was featured in the Millennium Project 2000 publication, *West Bromwich: A Century of Memories.* Her childhood memories when she was Lynne Sayers are also recounted in another poem, *Mill Street*, which has been read on a number of occasions as part of a Poetic Perambulation of West Bromwich.

Robin Pearson (INTRODUCTION) is a former one-time resident of The Lyng where he was involved in the Lyng History Project 1998-9. In 1999 he organised an exhibition and a Black Country Society walk to mark the centenary of Reuben Farley's death. He has had a number of books and map commentaries published on the history of various Black Country areas.

Richard Trainor (CHAPTER ONE) is an American scholar who undertook research into the industrial development of the Black Country. In particular he used the resources of Sandwell's local history collection which at that time was based in West Bromwich Library. He has held various academic posts at the universities of Oxford, Glasgow, and Greenwich before becoming Principal of London University's King's College. In 2010 he was awarded an honorary KBE.

FOREWORD
Pauline Lawley

IT WAS in 1978 that I first noticed Reuben Farley's grave. I had started a new job and took the "more interesting" route to Stone Cross via Heath Lane Cemetery. Walking past on a regular basis I began to notice the names on the impressive headstones lining the main path from the Heath Lane entrance. Here marked the final resting place of some very prominent West Bromwich people.

The first two monuments to draw my attention were those for brothers William and Joseph Lawley. I recognised their names immediately from the company they had founded, W. & J. Lawley in Sams Lane, as I had worked in the offices there for a few years in the sixties. So, if not in a hurry, I started to look at the names on the other headstones. That is when I spotted the burial place of Reuben Farley and his third wife Harriet Emily Farley, a double plot surrounded by grey granite edging stones with a large recumbent cross. Of course I had heard of Reuben Farley, after all, the town had the Farley Fountain, the Farley Clock Tower at Carters Green and Farley Park at Great Bridge but that was the limit of my knowledge of the man at that time. I did not know he had been Mayor five times, or that he was instrumental in acquiring the land for Dartmouth Park or indeed just how important he was to our town.

Some years later as a member of the West Bromwich Local History Society I started to do a little research into Reuben's life. Records revealed his driving force, his generosity, his involvement in all aspects of improving the town etc. but what of his private life? Where did he live, who were his wives, their families and connections?

Although greatly successful in most of his endeavours his family life appears to have been somewhat tinged with sadness. He came from quite a large family which was normal in Victorian times. He was still quite young when his father died and he stayed with his mother in the family home until his first marriage when he was in his forties. He would marry three times over the course of twenty years. His first two wives died childless and it would only be with his third wife Harriet (Fellows) that he would become a father himself when he was in his seventies.

Like his father before him Reuben would leave his bereaved wife with a young family to raise. There were five children aged from 11 to just 3 years old.

FOREWORD
Anne Wilkins

URING AUGUST 2000 I became interested in the history of West Bromwich Town Hall and my research made me aware of Alderman Reuben Farley, our town's great benefactor and first Mayor of West Bromwich.

The name of Farley was already known to me through a high triangular piece of land, known locally as Farley's Knob, which was situated within the boundaries of Addison Road, Asbury Road and the main Walsall Road, in Friar Park. This familiar landmark was often used to direct people to a specific road or building in the area.

However, that was not the end of my association with the Farley name for although at the time I was unaware of the fact, Reuben Farley's influence and benefaction to our town has touched upon many areas of my life. For example, in the 1950s I worked as a student nurse at the West Bromwich District Hospital. Many years later I discovered that Reuben Farley was not only a committee member of the new West Bromwich District Hospital Board but in his will he bequeathed £1,000 to its Endowment Fund.

Recent research has provided another surprise for me because I discovered that Mayor Reuben Farley had "well and truly laid" the Foundation Stone of St. Philip's Church, Beeches Road, where I was baptised.

My research for this book is based on inscribed trowels and keys presented to West Bromwich Civic Collection by Reuben Farley's daughter, Miss Margaret Farley.

AUTHORS' NOTES

WITH A keen interest in local history and especially local people who have had an impact on the development of West Bromwich we decided to bring together in one book, information from various sources on the life of Reuben Farley. Our first and five times Mayor.

We are pleased to begin with the article Dr. Carl Chinn did on Reuben in his series "Black Country People" for the *Express and Star* in 2008. Professor Chinn is well known locally in his role as an English Historian. He is Chair of Birmingham Community History, Department of History, University of Birmingham.

This is followed by the work by 'Rick' Trainor. Professor Richard Trainor is currently the Principal and President of King's College, London.

The chapters that follow reveal what West Bromwich was like before Reuben was born, what his birthplace was like and the progress made during his lifetime. This information is taken from local newspapers of the day.

It is sad that many of the town's residents may not recognize his name today but Reuben Farley was a key player in most of the important events which happened in the town's development in the nineteenth century.

Although no longer residing in West Bromwich, it has been a pleasure to have continuing contact with descendents of the Farley family and we have dedicated the last chapter to the family research completed by Jonathan Farley who is the Great-great grandson of John Farley, Reuben's brother.

Dr. Tom Farley is the great grandson of Reuben and it is he who has provided us with the lovely family photographs.

Anne Wilkins and Pauline Lawley

Contents

CHAPTER THREE
A LEADING LOCAL FIGURE

CHAPTER FOUR
FARLEY IN HIS OWN WORDS

CHAPTER FIVE
FIRST AND FIVE TIMES MAYOR

CHAPTER SIX
HIS GOOD WORKS

Contemporary Reports on Foundation Stones, Parks and Bandstands 1876-1894

CHAPTER SEVEN
THE OAK HOUSE

CHAPTER EIGHT
EVERYBODY ACKNOWLEDGES HIS GOOD WORKS

CHAPTER NINE
A SUDDEN ENDING

CHAPTER TEN
THE FARLEY RESIDENCES

CHAPTER ELEVEN
HISTORY OF THE FARLEY FAMILY

CHAPTER ONE

Reuben Farley The Man Of West Bromwich

BLACK COUNTRY PEOPLE
by Carl Chinn

"THE NAMES THAT MAKE THE REGION GREAT"
Express & Star supplement 21.02.2008

Some names even now resonate with business prowess, economic power, social prestige and municipal endeavour, Reuben Farley of West Bromwich, Joseph William Sankey of Bilston, Noah Hingley of Netherton and Dudley, the Chances of Smethwick, the Manders of Wolverhampton and the Owens of Darlaston.

All of them were families that had become rich through industrialisation. They lived in grand houses, enjoyed prosperous lifestyles and had the money to do what they wanted when they wanted.

With an income way beyond even the most amazing dreams of the working people of the West Midlands, they could have easily withdrawn from the towns from which they had made their fortunes and abandoned the workers who had helped them to their wealth. They did not.

In contrast to so many multi-national firms today that have no loyalty to place and people and move their production to wherever they can pay the cheapest wages, these families did not cut and run with their money. They stayed in our region, engaging in local government becoming involved in charitable organisations and acting for the good of their fellow citizens who were not so fortunately circumstanced.

Their commitment to their own localities was often inspired by the teachings of John Wesley and by the preachings of radical Non-Conformists such as Charles Berry, Minister of the Queen Street Congregationalist Church in Wolverhampton from 1883-87, he was eloquent, charismatic, thoughtful and inspiring.

In particular Berry was devoted to the idea of a Civic Gospel, whereby the rich would enter public life and work on behalf of the poor – so that all men and women, irrespective of their class, could be raised to higher living standards. The impact of this Civic Gospel was felt as strongly in the towns of the Black Country as much as it was in Wolverhampton, Birmingham, Manchester and Leeds. Many leading manufacturers and businessmen threw themselves into municipal activities. Reuben Farley was one of the most notable. An Anglican, he was as committed to social action as was any Methodist Unitarian or Congregationalist. He bestrode the civic life of West Bromwich as if he were the Colossus bestriding the harbour of Rhodes.

Farley was typical of that small but crucial band of successful manufacturers that believed intensely in owing a duty to the locality from which their money was made.

According to the Free Press of 1883, from when he was a young man, Farley "unceasingly identified himself with all the principal movements having their object the progress and well-being of the town and its inhabitants". Born in Great Bridge, Farley's father died when he was five but by hard work and flair he became a success in business. He then devoted himself to the well being of the people of West Bromwich. The Improvement Commission was the body that mostly ran the town before it became incorporated as a borough in 1882 – when Reuben Farley was chosen as the first mayor. Under his leadership of the Commission West Bromwich had obtained its own gas works, gained Dartmouth Park, built its Town Hall and other civic structures and had adopted the Public Libraries Act on November 30, 1870. It was one of the first 50 places in the country to do so and was only the fifth in Staffordshire.

That was not the extent of Farley's remarkable commitment to the welfare of the people of West Bromwich. He bestowed the Oak House Museum to the municipality and was a county magistrate, the long serving President of the West Bromwich Building Society and a member of both the Board of Guardians and the first School Board locally.

Unsurprisingly Farley was honoured as the first freeman of West Bromwich for he had "by his own ability, energy, conscientious discharge of duty, together with his unvarying courtesy of demeanour, acquitted himself to the approbation of his fellow townsmen of all classes, without distinction of creed or party".

– oOo –

THE WEST BROMWICH BUILDING SOCIETY

Extract from *"From Little Acorns Grow"* by Carl Chinn

Although not one of the founders of the Society, Reuben Farley was one of the two members who audited the balance sheet which accompanied the earliest document pertaining to the West Bromwich – the Second Annual Report (31 May 1851). He did so again the next year, and, from 1858 until his retirement in 1897 he signed each annual report as President.

Farley stood out for his 'high sense of honour', 'stainless character' and 'steady zeal in the interest of religion, morality and benevolence'. Not least amongst his achievements was guiding the rapid growth of the West Bromwich so that it had a 'firm hold on the public'.

His tremendous contribution was acknowledged in 1898 when he retired as President. The annual meeting resolved unanimously to *'tender him its grateful thanks for the labour and attention he has given to the Society as its President for more than 40 years; they regret very much that while his interest and confidence in the Society continues unabated, his numerous engagements and advancing years constrain him to resign a position which he has honoured by his constant and careful attention'.*

IRONFOUNDER AND COALMASTER
by Richard Trainor

Reuben Farley's principal significance lies neither in his impressive business success nor in his foundation of a partially landed family. For Farley was a classic example of the many Victorian businessmen who were active and influential leaders in the public affairs of industrial towns.

Reuben Farley was born in West Bromwich, Staffordshire, on 27 January 1826, the eighth of ten children of the mining engineer Thomas Farley (1781-1830) and Elizabeth (1792-1885), daughter of John Llewelyn. Like other future local leaders, Farley was a day pupil at the local Borwicks Heath Academy and an active member of the West Bromwich Institution for the Advancement of Knowledge. This schooling helped Farley to give speeches that were erudite as well as fluent and to display 'intellectual abilities of no mean order' {1}.

Having been apprenticed to a local mining surveyor on leaving school, Farley took over the Dunkirk Colliery when he was twenty-one. He later added at least one other pit in association with his first wife's family. Farley also owned some brickworks. His principal involvement in unincorporated firms, however, lay in ironfounding. By 1861, in partnership with his sister's husband, George Taylor, Farley was able to purchase the local Summit Foundry, which became the core of the firm of Taylor & Farley. Twenty years later Farley bought his late brother-in-law's share and became sole proprietor.

During the later nineteenth century, as Black Country ironfounding expanded in the wake of the decline of the basic iron industry, the company grew rapidly and became 'one of the largest of its kind in South Staffordshire' {2}. Taylor & Farley's rolls and other mill and forge machines were well known throughout the major iron and steel districts and the firm won a medal at the 1897 Brussels Exhibition.

Farley remained the active head of Taylor & Farley, which occupied much of his time. Nevertheless, his experience and connections were much valued in boardrooms, and Farley played a leading role in several of the large limited companies which became significant, though still atypical, features of the area's economy from the 1870s. Farley was both a leading shareholder and chairman in two private corporations – Fellows, Morton & Clayton, a large canal carrier which his brother-in-law Joshua Fellows had founded, and Edwin Danks & Co., an important local maker of boilers and boats. Farley was also influential in two public companies which encountered major technical and financial problems while pioneering large-scale, deep-shaft mining on the south eastern side of the Black Country. A promoter and director of the Sandwell Park Colliery Co., Farley later became disaffected. He was an active chairman, however, of the Hamstead Colliery Co and represented the firms at regional meetings of coalmasters.

Through these commitments, together with his chairmanship of the South Staffordshire Ironfounders Association, his involvement in other employers' organisations and his personal ties to key businessmen in the district, Farley became one of the leading figures in the industrial life of the Black Country {3}. Moreover, although he made no claims to national prominence, Farley was an original member of the Iron and Steel Institute. Nor was he a cipher in the field of labour relations. Here many of Farley's attitudes were stern. No friend to 'grandmotherly legislation' {4} he condemned the eight-hour day as 'interference with the liberty of the subject'{5}. Farley also criticised union organisers for alienating employers from workmen. Still, though embattled at Hamstead, Farley evidently experienced little labour trouble in his own firm, where he provided excursions and pensions.

Farley was perceived locally as a 'self-made man' whose position was 'entirely due to his meritorious conduct, integrity, and ability' {6}. Yet while the probate value of his estate, £167,735 represented a significant improvement on his father's social position, Farley's early acquisitions suggest that, like many upwardly mobile Victorian businessmen, he started his career with substantial assets in hand. Furthermore, Farley was less a brilliant innovator or manager than someone adept at pooling capital with other businessmen. Farley was an exacting negotiator who nonetheless won good will through his 'genial disposition and courteous bearing' {7}.

Each of Farley's wives – Hannah Duce (m 1867; d 1876), Elizabeth Haines (m 1879; d 1885) and Harriette Fellows (m 1887; d 1938) – came from an important Black Country business family. His last spouse bore him five children; the youngest was born when Farley was seventy.

Business success allowed Farley to collect paintings and to travel. Late in life he also acquired and improved a substantial house in West Bromwich where he was determined to continue to reside. If Farley deliberately eschewed 'gentrification' his sons grasped it eagerly. They were educated at Uppingham, and in two cases, at Cambridge; the eldest had an estate in Huntingdonshire, while the two younger sons lived in rural Warwickshire. Nevertheless the latter became actively involved in Taylor & Farley after 1918.

Farley's contributions were modest in the relatively contentious fields of religion and partisan politics, where his early enthusiasms waned. At first an active Wesleyan, Farley converted to Anglicanism by the 1860s. He remained devout, served as a churchwarden and led the 'Church Party' in the first School Board election in West Bromwich in 1871. Yet Farley subsequently avoided sectarian disputes; he refused to stand for re-election to the School Board, remained friendly with many Nonconformists and continued to patronise Dissenting as well as Anglican causes.

In politics Farley was a keen Liberal early in his adult life. By 1868 however, he had distanced himself from the 'advanced' Liberals of the neighbourhood, whose enthusiasm for religious controversy and protection of trade unions was increasing. Farley, desiring 'less of Party and more of Patriotism' (speech on Parliament), was an inactive Liberal Unionist from 1886. Many fellow townsmen had urged him to stand for parliament when West Bromwich acquired its own seat a year earlier. However, like many other Victorian businessmen heavily involved with local affairs, Farley declined the opportunity.

Instead, he channelled his formidable energies into the municipal and philanthropic betterment of his native town. A firm believer in the Black Country's belated but vigorous version of the 'civic gospel' found elsewhere in cities such as Birmingham, Farley felt obliged to 'make the lives of the people brighter and happier'{8}. He thought that civic improvement would also assist prosperity and would prevent both business irresponsibility and excessive demands by working men. In addition, Farley no doubt aspired to the social prominence he achieved as 'the foremost figure in the public life of the town' {9}.

Farley was a county magistrate from 1879 and one of the first borough JPs of West Bromwich. An active Poor Law guardian in the 1850s and 1860s, Farley, like many leading businessmen, later abandoned that particularly troubled sphere of local administration in order to concentre on municipal affairs. He served for eight years as chairman of the West Bromwich Improvement Commissioners, took a leading role in their provision of local amenities, and defeated Joseph Chamberlain in a battle for control of the town's gas supply. When West Bromwich was incorporated in 1882 Farley's was the only name suggested for the mayor's chair. He filled it four more times and received particular credit for discouraging partisanship in council affairs.

Throughout his local government career Farley proved especially adept at promoting prestigious projects – such as municipal utilities and civic buildings – through which the Black Country's local authorities compensated for their patchy record in providing basic services such as sanitation.

Voluntary societies as diverse as the Rifle Volunteers, friendly societies, a choral society and West Bromwich Albion Football Club found Farley an active officer and major contributor. For a quarter-century he attended almost every committee meeting of the West Bromwich Building Society and he bequeathed £1000 to the district hospital, on whose 'weekly board' he had served for thirty-one years. Farley also assisted co-ordination between philanthropy and local government, notably by promoting technical education.

Having developed a close relationship with the Fifth Earl of Dartmouth, Farley played a key role in Lord Dartmouth's gift to the town of its major park. Farley himself gave West Bromwich both a recreation ground and a museum. Such facilities, he thought, would allow 'all classes and sections of the community' to meet 'on common neutral ground' {10}.

Farley did not escape criticism, especially from those sections of the lower middle class and working class which argued that his projects pressed too hard on small ratepayers. Yet he learned to compromise, thus enabling his own plans to prevail, albeit in modified form. Moreover, Farley remained personally popular, even among his opponents, for his generosity, honesty and tactfulness – and as a symbol of the town's rapid economic and social progress during his lifetime. West

Bromwich made Farley its first freeman in 1896 and erected a clock tower in his honour a year later. At Farley's death, the mayor, a former critic, ordered public mourning; 'thousands of humbler citizens' {11} attended the funeral.

Having confined his activities primarily to his home locality, Farley helped to complement the regional emphasis of wealthier and more cosmopolitan colleagues such as Sir Alfred Hickman. Farley's unusually protracted and diverse public service only exaggerated a general, if by the 1890s a declining, tendency for prosperous Victorian businessmen to exert themselves in the public affairs of the localities from which they drew their substantial profits. Men like Farley had especially great impact in medium-sized towns, such as those in the Black Country, where civic life was poorly developed until the later nineteenth century. Their interventions helped replace the disputed edicts of earlier nineteenth century local leaders with the less absolute but more accepted decisions of the quasi-democratic 1890s.

Farley died in West Bromwich on 11 March 1899, having attended a public meeting less than a fortnight earlier.

A successful entrepreneur and an effective business leader, Farley was especially influential as a civic dignitary. By concentrating on relatively uncontroversial 'improvements' Farley typified the increasingly conciliatory and progressive leadership of the late nineteenth century Black Country elites.

From: D.J. Jeremy (ed)
Dictionary of Business Biography 40/2
(London: Butterworths, 1984)

{1}   Jewell (1893) 16.
{2}   West Bromwich Chronicle 20 Nov 1896.
{3}   Birmingham Daily Mail 13 Mar 1899.
{4}   Staffordshire RO D888/1 27 May 1897.
{5}   Birmingham Daily Post 3 February 1891.
{6}   Free Press 24 Mar 1883.
{7}   Birmingham Daily Mail 13 Mar 1899.
{8}   Weekly News 25 April 1896.
{9}   Free Press 17 Mar 1899.
{10} Free Press 8 May 1886.
{11} West Bromwich Chronicle 15 Mar 1899.

FAMILY CONNECTIONS
THROUGH BUSINESS AND MARRIAGE

The Taylor Family

Reuben's sister Susannah married Ironfounder George Taylor in 1833. Their daughters Emily and Mary were witnesses at Reuben's first marriage.

George, Susannah and their children moved from Golds Green to Carters Green and finally to Grove Vale, Great Barr.

Reuben and George formed a successful business partnership. They owned the Dunkirk Colliery from the mid 1850s to about 1870 and acquired the Summit Foundry by 1861 where they manufactured all types of rolls for the iron trade. By 1881 George had retired and Reuben took over the Taylor & Farley business which continued to be run by the Farley family until the 1940s.

THE LONDON GAZETTE 3 OCTOBER, 1941 (REF5739)
TAYLOR & FARLEY LIMITED

NOTICE *is hereby given that at an Extraordinary General Meeting of Taylor & Farley Limited duly convened and held at the registered office of the Company, Summit Foundry West Bromwich, on Tuesday the 23rd day of September 1941 at 2 o'clock in the afternoon the following Resolution was passed as a Special Resolution:*
"That the Company be wound up voluntarily and that Mr. Robert William Rutledge of 131 Edmund Street, Birmingham be appointed Liquidator for the purposes of such winding-up."
Dated this 23rd day of September, 1941.
Reuben Ll. Farley, Chairman

The Taylor & Farley offices building still stands today on Kenrick Way.
Photograph supplied by Dr. Tom Farley

The Duce Family

Reuben's first marriage at the age of 42 was to Hannah Duce, daughter of Gun Lock Manufacturer John Duce and his wife Esther. In 1841 the Duce family were living in Church Street, Wednesbury with ten children listed on the census return. By the time of her marriage to Reuben, Hannah's father had died and her brother John Taylor Duce had taken over the family business. Several members of the family then lived close to each other in Bridge Street and in 1880 two entries appeared in Kelly's Directory of Staffordshire for John Taylor Duce & Sons;

GUN LOCK MAKERS of Church Hill Wednesbury.
WINE & SPIRIT MERCHANTS of 23 Bridge Street
and Market Place Wednesbury.

To this day the Market Place building still stands with the name John Taylor Duce and Sons built into the façade. A lasting reminder of a prominent family from the Victorian era.

*A Farley & Duce business connection existed through the Whyley Colliery at West Bromwich from about 1871 to its close around 1883. Also the Cutler's End Colliery from about 1876 to 1886.

Hannah was 38 years of age when she married Reuben. They lived at 14 New Street but their marriage would only last for nine years. In 1876, possibly in an effort to improve her failing health, Hannah was staying at 6 Beacon Terrace, Torquay, a Georgian building overlooking the sea and the harbour side where she sadly died on December 10th, aged 47. The main cause of death was recorded as Phthisis Pulmonalis (an archaic term for Tuberculosis). Reuben was with her when she died.

    She was buried at Christ Church, West Bromwich.

Here sleepeth Hannah the Beloved Wife of Reuben Farley
Who entered into rest at Torquay on December 10th 1876 age 47.
As for me, I will behold thy face in righteousness:
I shall be satisfied when I awake, with thy likeness.
Psalm 17

*mines information supplied by Dennis Neale, Black Country Muse.

The Haines Family

Reuben's second marriage was to Elizabeth Haines the daughter of Job Haines (deceased) who had been a Coal and Iron Master and Magistrate for the County of Stafford. At 54 years of age Reuben was 17 years older than Elizabeth. Three of her siblings were witnesses: Brother Richard, sisters Ann Haines and Mary Fellows together with William Henry Salter (of another important West Bromwich family) and Ellen Duce (sister of Reuben's first wife).

Marriage Announcement Thursday April 17, 1879. *The Birmingham Daily Post*
"The Marriage of Mr. Reuben Farley, chairman of the Board of Commissioners, to Miss Elizabeth Haines, of Hill House, West Bromwich took place yesterday. The ceremony was performed at the parish church (All Saints) by the Rev. R. Hodgson, M.A. assisted by the Rev. F. Willett, M.A. and the Rev. G.R. Chell, M.A. (brother-in-law of the bride). The event created unusual interest and flags were freely displayed in different parts of the town. The presents to the bride were numerous and costly. In testimony of the respect in which Mr. Farley is held by his work people, the employees of Summit Foundry presented him with a silver epergne, of Messrs. Elkington's manufacture, upon which was engraved a suitable inscription. The colliers and others engaged at the Whyley and Cutler's End Collieries also presented him with a valuable timepiece. The gratifying feature of these presentations is that every man and boy connected with Mr. Farley's works and collieries contributed with hearty good will. Merry peals were rung during the day at various churches in the town in honour of the event. As the wedding party left the church a charming little girl, daughter of one of the foundry foremen, stepped forward from the crowd and presented the bride with a bouquet. To celebrate the event the Summit Foundry workpeople were entertained by Mr. Farley to dinner last evening in the large room of the Rose and Crown Inn, West Bromwich."

The Haines family lived in the Great Bridge/Horseley Heath area. When Job Haines died in January 1868 his sons Richard and John carried on the family business. The 1871 census listed Richard as BA Oxford, Coalmaster employing 50 men and 8 boys.

Reuben's marriage to Elizabeth was even shorter than that to Hannah. After just 6 years Reuben was with Elizabeth when she died at their New Street home on September 25, 1885. Dr. Thomas Underhill certified that the death was due to Heart Disease (8 months) Albuminuria (7 months).

In affectionate remembrance of
ELIZABETH
The dearly loved wife of REUBEN FARLEY
who died 25th Sept 1885 aged 43
Come unto me and I will give you rest

Just seven months earlier Reuben's mother Elizabeth had also died. She was 92 years of age. Both of these important women in his life were buried at Christ Church with first wife Hannah.

Also sacred to the ELIZABETH widow of THOMAS
Who died 21st Feb 1885 aged 92.
In grateful memory of a mothers worth
her gentleness and goodness
her faith and meekness

her patient countenance in all
that is lovely and of good report.
He that believe in me said the Lord, though he were dead, yet shall he live.

The Fellows Family

Reuben was in his sixties when he married Harriette 33, daughter of James Fellows. Harriette was born on May 7, 1854 just ten days before her father died at the age of 49. He had worked as an agent for a canal carrier before deciding to start his own company in 1837. It was not long before the company grew and he moved his operation to Tipton in 1841. His wife Eliza was left to carry on the business until son Joshua was old enough to take over and he became the driving force of the business and its expansion. Long distance canal carrying was the mainstay of the business in the early days and the next few years saw various partnerships set up with other carriers.

In 1876 Joshua Fellows and Frederick Morton came together to form Fellows, Morton & Co. and in 1889 William Clayton merged with them to become Fellows, Morton & Clayton Ltd. Three managing directors were appointed, Joshua Fellows, Frederick Morton and Thomas Clayton. Alderman Reuben Farley was placed as chairman and the shareholders comprised mainly of family members of the Managing Directors.

So Reuben's third wife Harriette Emily Fellows also

Joshua Fellows.

came from a successful business family with her brother Joshua being one of the most respected leaders of the canal transportation industry. The term used for boats built by or for Fellows, Morton & Clayton was 'Joshers' after Joshua.

As well as John Fellows and Mary Eleanor Fellows as witnesses to the marriage was G.H. Claughton another important man of his day. He was Mayor of Dudley four times from 1891-1895. He also dealt with Reuben's will as the index of Wills & Administrations shows that probate was granted to Gilbert Henry Claughton (together with Rev Newton Theodore Langley) on May 26, 1899.

Reuben and Harriette had five children.

She died on August 31, 1938 aged 84 at Wornditch Hall, Kimbolton and is buried with Reuben in Heath Lane Cemetery. Through marriage the Haines, Fellows and Farley families were connected over many years:

Two daughters of Job and Mary Haines married two brothers from the Fellows family and a third daughter married Reuben Farley.

1857 Mary Haines   married Joshua Fellows
1864 Sarah Lees Haines   married William Henry Fellows
1879 Elizabeth Haines   married Reuben Farley
1887 the marriage of Reuben Farley to Harriette Emily Fellows (sister to Joshua & William)

The 1871 to 1891 census returns showed that Mary and Joshua Fellows lived at Churchfield House. In 1881 Harriet was recorded at the address too.

(It was in the grounds of this house that Joshua Fellows and a number of prominent gentlemen resident in West Bromwich opened the first golf course in the town in 1895.)

By 1879 the Haines family had moved into historic Hill House a short distance away as this was Elizabeth's address when she married Reuben. In 1881 widowed Mary Haines was listed there with three of her adult children. This was the West Bromwich residence of James Eaton during his final years. He was midshipman on the *Temeraire* during the Battle of Trafalgar and passed on Nelson's famous message "England Expects That Every Man will do His Duty". Eaton was buried at All Saints Church in 1857.

The Three Marriages

21st August 1867   *St. John's Church in the Parish of Wednesbury*

Reuben Farley	42	batchelor	Iron Founder & Coal Master West Bromwich father: Thomas Farley, Mine Agent
Hannah Duce	38	spinster	of Wednesbury Father: John Duce, Gun Lock Manufacturer
Witnesses:			Thomas Bill, William Marsh, Susan Moore, Elizabeth Adams, Emily Taylor, Mary Anne Elizabeth Amelia Taylor

16th April, 1879   *The Parish Church of West Bromwich (All Saints)*

Reuben Farley	full	widower	Coal master & Ironfounder West Bromwich father: Thomas Farley, Mining Engineer (dead)
Elizabeth Haines	full	spinster	of West Bromwich Father: Job Haines, Coal & Iron Master (dead)
Witnesses:			Richard Haines, Ann Haines, W.H. Salter, Ellen Duce, Mary Fellows

19th October, 1887   *The Parish Church of Sedgley*

Reuben Farley	full	widower	Ironfounder/Colliery Proprietor, West Bromwich Father: Thomas Farley, Mining Engineer
Harriette Emily Fellows	full	spinster	of Sedgley Father: James Fellows, Canal Carrier
Witnesses:			G.H. Claughton, John Fellows, Mary Eleanor Fellows

THE CHILDREN OF REUBEN AND HARRIETTE FARLEY

Reuben was in his sixties when he and Harriette had the first of their five children who were all born in West Bromwich.

Edith Margaret Farley was their first child, born November 9, 1888. She never married and died in Harbury at the age of 87 on January 5, 1976.

Reuben Llewellyn Farley, O.B.E. their first son, was born June 26, 1890 and was educated at Uppingham and Trinity College, Cambridge. At the beginning of WW1 he seems to have enlisted in the Cavalry as the September 8, 1914 edition of *The London Gazette* includes him in a list of "temporary Second Lieutenants". His medal records list the theatre of war as France in March 1915 with the 3rd Hussars. He gained his Aeronaut's (Balloonist) Certificate on March 10, 1916 with the Royal Flying Corps which had been formed in 1912. *The Flight Journal of May 3, 1917* included Major R.L. Farley, R.F.C. in the list of wounded.

The London Gazette of May 30, 1919 published a *Supplement on Tuesday June 3, 1919* announcing the King's Birthday Honours List which included Major (A./Lt.Col) Reuben Llewelyn Farley (Cavly. Res) as an Officer of the Military Division of the Most Excellent Order of the British Empire.

The London Gazette of October 3, 1939 included his name in the list of those granted commissions for the duration of hostilities as Pilot Officers on probation on September 29, 1939. The Forces War Records listed him with the 3rd Huntingdonshire Battalion of the T.A. Home Guard in 1941. He was still listed with the Territorial Army Associations, Huntingdon Battalion in January 1942.

It was about 1920 when he bought Wornditch Hall, Kimbolton and in later years he would serve as a JP and High Sheriff of Cambridgeshire and Huntingdonshire. In 1952 he was entered in Burkes Landed Gentry as 'Farley of Wornditch Hall, Kimbolton, Huntingdonshire'. Never marrying, he died March 18, 1954 aged 63 at 35 Weymouth Street, London.

Charles Finch Farley, M.C. was born September 3, 1892. Like his brother he too was educated at Uppingham and Trinity College, Cambridge. He was a Captain in the 4th Dragoon Guards and awarded the Military Cross.

The Supplement to the London Gazette, July 26, 1918 listed the award:
"Capt. Charles Finch Farley, Dn. Gds.

For conspicuous gallantry and devotion when in command of a regimental working party. After an hour's intense bombardment the enemy attacked, being held on the immediate front, but gaining their objectives on the right and left. With the greatest courage and skill he continued to hold his line and with the help of a machine gun and Hotchkiss rifle to inflict great losses on the enemy passing around his right rear. He maintained his position till it was shelled by our own guns, when he withdrew his command, fighting step by step".

His marriage to Mavis Loftus Tottenham on September 18, 1919 produced two children, Pamela Margaret Farley and Anne Dorothea Farley. He lived for some years at 'Avonside' Barford, Warwickshire. There was a second marriage to Barbara Joan Walter in February 1961. This was eight years before his death in Harbury, Leamington Spa in September 1969 aged 76.

Clara Helena Fellows Farley who was born August 21, 1894 appears to be named after her mother's sister. Clara was a member of the Red Cross VAD (Voluntary Aid Detachment) and was listed as a VAD nurse at the VAD hospital, Sandy in the *Supplement to the London Gazette 19 January, 1920*. 'VADs' were trained in first aid and nursing to provide supplementary aid to the Territorial Forces Medical Service during the war. She married Major Edward Guy Wood on July 12, 1920 in Sandy, Bedfordshire. They had five children.

Clara died on December 26, 1995 aged 101.

Francis Dashwood Farley C.B.E. was born June 19, 1896 and educated at Uppingham. He was a Lieutenant in the Royal Leicester Regiment 5th Battalion (Territorial) during WW1.

His medals record shows the "Theatre of War first served in France". He was Justice of the Peace for Warwickshire in 1941, Deputy Lieutenant of Warwickshire in 1954 and vice-chairman of the Warwickshire County Council between 1956 and 1958.

'Alderman Francis Dashwood Farley, J.P., Chairman, Warwickshire Police Authority' was made an Ordinary Commander of the Civil Division of the Most Excellent Order of the British Empire in 1965. *(Supplement to the London Gazette, January 1, 1965)*

Francis married Winifred Joan Davis on February 8, 1921 and they had two children, Richard Dashwood Farley in 1922 (who would marry three times) and John Dashwood Farley in 1925 (the father of Thomas William Dashwood Farley born October 1962).

Francis died on June 29, 1966 aged 70 at Warwick Hospital.

CHAPTER TWO

Early Days

EARLY WEST BROMWICH

From J.W.A. Aston's book 'The Story of West Bromwich' it is possible to get a good idea of what early West Bromwich was like.

Before the Industrial Revolution

In the mid-fourteenth century the small Bromwich village consisted of thirty to forty houses radiating from the church, trodden paths through the grass would lead to each peasant's house. Some of the larger houses were now being roughly enclosed to give private ground forming a small garden for growing vegetables, herbs and possibly a fruit tree. The smaller houses inhabited by the poorer class would have only a very small plot of ground, barely enough room for cabbages and onions and only occasionally would one come across a pig or a few fowl. By the time Elizabeth I came to the throne (1559) West Bromwich was just a typical country village with a number of farms and labourers cottages and a large heath surrounded by small houses.

By 1802 an Act of Parliament was obtained dividing up West Bromwich Heath which at the time was estimated at 387 acres. The parish was a group of houses surrounding the heath and crossed by a turnpike road. It was said at one time in the old coaching days that the wildest part of the entire journey from London to Holyhead was across Bromwich Heath! After the heath was enclosed houses began to spring up and soon a town emerged.

Large factories were not yet to play a great part in industrial life. The family at home were still the backbone of the Black Country industry. Every member of the family worked from a living at home. They worked from dawn to dusk.

During Reuben's Lifetime

By 1831 the census showed that West Bromwich had taken the lead among Black Country towns as far as growth was concerned and by 1834 gas lighting was installed the whole length of the main road from Birmingham to Dartmouth Square. Although the nail trade was in trouble, the Midlands was making its mark throughout the world because of the Black Country iron. From 1855 to 1865 the peak of the iron trade was reached. Cannons were being made at Tipton and Bilston, gun barrels, locks and pistols at West Bromwich.

West Bromwich was recognised as a Municipal Borough in 1882 and was granted County Borough Status in 1890. The town could now go ahead with improvements without having to refer to the county council. The period from 1875 to the outbreak of WW1 was one of chronic poverty, the workhouses were generally always full and sometimes paupers had to be boarded-out by the Guardians of the Workhouse because there just wasn't enough room to house everybody. By this time West Bromwich was no longer the village of a few hamlets that it had been for centuries. The population had now exploded from 15300 in 1831 to 65100 in 1901.

CHILDHOOD MEMORIES OF EMILY IZON

When Emily Izon was 82 years of age she wrote an account of her own childhood for her grandchildren entitled, 'Grandmama's Childhood'. W.E. Jephcott, in his 65th article on Old West Bromwich (09/06/1944) referred to it as, *"A narrative which gives an intimate picture of life in the area before it had become the Black Country and when West Bromwich was still a green and pleasant rural place, when its few works were only incidental features of the landscape and before the colliery spoil banks and furnace slag heaps had defaced it".*

Emily Izon was a daughter of William Izon, of The Lodge on West Bromwich Heath. Her story contains many interesting glimpses of life as it was lived in West Bromwich in the 1820s by children of the well-to-do classes.

She wrote:

> *"There were no railways and very few coaches when we were young, at least when we were children and therefore people stayed at home for many months at a time and didn't complain of the dullness of the country as they do now. The first time we went to the seaside – a rare event – we drove all the way in our own carriage, a distance of about 120 miles. We also drove all the way to London and it took three days to perform the journey, stopping at hotels for two or three nights. But it was to me a delightful journey staying at the old-fashioned country inns and rural villages until we came to that smoky crowded city which I was then so glad to leave and return to our quiet and beloved home.*
>
> *Our pleasant visit over, we came back to our lessons and governess, for we had regular hours for school work and had to say our lessons with a book poised on our heads to keep us upright and if the book fell down we lost one 'good mark'. No one was allowed to stoop and there was another fine if we put our elbows on the table. Stooping and what was called 'lolling' were punishable offences. Schools were terribly severe places in those days and the golden rule for all children then was this 'Children should be seen but not heard'.*

Boys of the working classes touched their caps and girls curtseyed when they met or were spoken to by the gentry. Respect to our superiors was then a universal law. I wish that it was so now.

All are gone now; the fields where we played are turned into streets and a Town Hall, Market Hall and many public buildings cover the land where the dear old home once stood and the pleasant grounds and garden around it."

— oOo —

The Lodge estate was sold after the death of William Izon, some of the land being bought by the West Bromwich Commissioners for public purposes and other portions by private individuals for the erection of houses. The Lodge was demolished in 1868. The same year 30 acres of wheat, barley and oats, hayricks, farm implements, horses and cattle were sold by auction and the Lodge colliery the following year.

LOOKING BACK

In 1899, the year Reuben Farley died, Lavinia Benbow published her book 'The Old Oak House', A Tale of the Seventeenth Century. This is a novel of the English Civil War in the West Midlands including the Battle on Camp Hill and the Siege of Dudley Castle, centred on the Oak House, West Bromwich.

She dedicated the book to Reuben:

To The Memory of
Our Beloved And Generous Fellow-Townsman,
The Late Alderman Reuben Farley, J.P.
This Book is Gratefully dedicated by the Author

Born in West Bromwich in c1851 Lavinia was the daughter of John and Ann Holland of Kenrick Street. She married Pryce Benbow, a grocer, in 1869. For many years they lived in Lodge Road and would have witnessed the building of the Town Hall and neighbouring buildings.

In her book she looks back from the Victorian town of 1899:

"If the men and women who lived in the village of Bromwych about two hundred and fifty years ago could be permitted to return for a short time, and to gaze on the busy manufacturing hive in which we are living at the close of this wonderful nineteenth century, it would not be surprising if, with a bewildered look and an emphatic shake of the head, they denied ever having seen the place before.

They would see what in their day were great wooded stretches, green pastures, and smiling cornfields, covered over with vast manufactories that are known all over the civilised world, or with miles of houses where busy workers live.

They would see what was once a lonely, wide-stretching heath, covered over with all kinds of flourishing business premises; with large public buildings where honoured citizens meet to discuss the best ways of governing the busy town; and with others used for the nursing of the sick and maimed. They would see large public schools, both elementary and advanced, where the poorest child may receive knowledge, which, if rightly applied, will enable him to do his part towards maintaining his country's greatness, and building up his own character and fortune.

They would see many churches, in addition to the one in which they had loved to worship, dotted about, their towers and pinnacles seeming to point men's thoughts to a higher life, and in which their descendants are able to worship God according to their own faith, none daring to make them afraid.

It would only be by taking them to one or two well-preserved bits, that we should hope to convince them that it was the place where they had lived their span of earthly life."

If she too could be permitted to return for a short time what would her description of the town be now?

VICTORIAN TRAVEL

Born in the early nineteenth century, Reuben Farley would experience changes in the transport system that would transform the Victorian's world.

The journey to London before 1837 was regarded as an undertaking of great magnitude. From Reuben's own reminiscences we know that it took his mother fourteen hours to make the journey from their Great Bridge home to Birmingham (by gig) then on to London by the mail coach. It was horsepower or nothing! Such travel by coach on turnpike roads was slow but things were about to change thanks to steam power.

Once railways were established as the newest and fastest communication and transport system it had great social, political and economic effects on the whole country.

So how exciting it must have been for Reuben, as an eleven-year-old boy, to witness the first train through Newton Road railway station in July 1837.

"My godfather, Mr. Francis Finch, M.P. for Walsall, lived at the Hollies, Great Barr in those days and Mrs. Finch kindly invited my mother, two little sisters and myself to spend the day with her at Barr in order to see the train pass through Newton Road and the Barr Meadows. It appeared to me a most wonderful sight to see carriages going along without horses and made an impression on my mind which I shall never forget."

Reuben was not averse to make long journeys to represent the interests of his town. When the West Bromwich Commissioners petitioned Parliament against the 1875 Birmingham Gas Bill he travelled to Westminster. September 1890 saw him travel even further afield when he attended a meeting of the Iron & Steel Institute in America. He travelled on the White Star Line ship *Majestic* to New York. Reuben and J.H. Pearson were two of the Staffordshire Ironmasters who reported back with their impressions as to the trade and tariffs in the U.S.A. The Americans had simply copied English methods but had a tendency to do things on a much bigger scale and the two men were particularly impressed by their visit to the 'Edgar Thompson' works of Andrew Carnegie in Pittsburg.

CHAPTER THREE

A Leading Local Figure

PREDECESSORS OF THE TOWN COUNCIL

In April 1943 W.E. Jephcott wrote (as part of his series on Old West Bromwich) about what the town was like in the 1870s. Taking information from a Directory of 1872 he recalled the people who were then prominent in the public and social life of the town.

> *"There is always a great interest in personalities.*
> *After all, the real life of a town is in its*
> *residents much more than in its buildings."*

The principal public body was the Board of Improvement Commissioners, forerunner of the Town Council and discharging (though in a more limited degree) the same functions. It consisted of 16 members and held its general meetings once a month at the offices. These were in the building at the corner of New Street and Pitt Street. The main entrance was a large doorway in New Street.

The chairman was *Peter Duckworth Bennett who carried on business as an ironfounder in Houghton Street, Spon Lane, under the title of Peter Duckworth Bennett and Co. They produced heavy castings and a sample of their manufactures is the massive lamp which originally stood in the centre of Dartmouth Square. When the present clock was substituted the lamp was moved to Stone Cross at the centre of the junction of the streets there. Other Commissioners were:

Thomas Davis J.P. an Ironmaster with works at Golds Hill who resided at The Hollies, Hill Top. He was also chairman of the School Board.

John Arthur Kenrick J.P. of the famous Spon Lane firm of ironfounders; joint founder of Kenrick and Jefferson Ltd.

Henry Williams, J.P. who lived at Highfields. He was an iron merchant who started in Oak Road but later removed to the corner of Paradise Street and the station drive. He was also captain-commandant of the West Bromwich Rifle Volunteers.

William Burch who was a chemist in High Street, next to Hudson's passage. The directory says that he was also in charge of the Fire Station, the keys of which were kept at his shop. The Fire Station then was in the passage leading off the High Street to Hudson's works. The fire equipment consisted of a manual engine in which the pumping was done by men standing on either side of the engine and pushing up and down the long bars which worked the pump.

Brownlow William Blades, brick-maker. He was for many years a member of the Board of Guardians and the School Board. His brother Alderman J.H. Blades became the first M.P. for West Bromwich in 1885 when the town was separated from the Wednesbury Division and created a Parliamentary Borough with its own representative in the Commons.

Samuel Lees of J.B.& S. Lees, iron manufacturers and timber merchants. He became Mayor in November 1889 and died in December 13, 1890 while occupying the Mayoral chair for a second year.

Edward Caddick, solicitor, who was then in partnership with his brother Alfred in New Street. Alfred became the first Town Clerk of the borough.

Thomas Lloyd who carried on business as a butcher in New Street.

Reuben Farley, one of the town's greatest benefactors and its first Mayor.

John Field, a mining engineer who lived at Hill Top and was associated with the Sandwell Park Colliery Company. He served for many years as a Guardian.

Samuel Roberts who lived at the Grange, Carters Green, and with his brother John carried on the famous business of J & S Robert, Ironfounders. Their works were originally next to Christ Church on the ground occupied by the Post Office and the smoke from their furnaces caused the stonework of the church to assume its black hue. Later the business was moved to Swan Village.

Thomas Rollason, who was a land and mine surveyor, lived in Barrows Street and was the third occupier of the Mayoral chair.

Dr. John Manley, later the Medical Officer of Health, then a private practitioner.

William Henry Salter, who lived at Oakley Cottage, Roebuck Lane.

Joshua Fellows lived at Churchfield.

The clerk to the Commissioners from 1865 to 1882 was **Charles H. Bayley,** solicitor, who resided at The Larches, Paradise Street. He died the very year that the town became a borough. He was fond of literary pursuits, particularly antiquarian and archaeological, and collected much information for a history of West Bromwich. He printed some publications with his own private press.

*Peter Duckworth Bennett.   **W.E. Jephcott 07.01.1944**
Peter Duckworth Bennett for some years resided at a large house in Halford Lane behind the Smethwick end of the Albion ground. It was demolished after the last war and the site developed by Smethwick Corporation as a housing estate. In the

grounds was a large fig tree, possibly the only one in the district and also a splendid acacia. They may have been relics of the period when Pope's Nurseries occupied the site of the Albion's playing pitch.

A tragic end befell Peter Duckworth Bennett at the age of 60. On November 28, 1885 the then Prince of Wales (later King Edward VII) came to Birmingham to open the Jaffray Hospital and the New Art Gallery. Mr. Bennett was a guest at a Mayoral luncheon at the Council House and when the Prince was about to drive away, Mr. Bennett and several other guests went on the roof of the portico in front to witness his departure. A player in the orchestra also went there and being in danger of falling, clutched at the nearest man who happened to be Mr. Bennett.

This caused the latter to fall through the glass of a skylight onto the pavement nearly 50 feet below. His injuries were not severe but the shock was so great that he died in less than 20 minutes.

GUARDIANS OF THE POOR

Chartist "Barber Wilkes" 1786-1874.   **W.E. Jephcott 1943**

During his lifetime Reuben Farley became a notable man much loved and respected by the people of West Bromwich but an antagonist of the young Farley was another man who was popular with the townspeople. He was George Wilkes (b1786) who in later years was known locally as 'Barber Wilkes'. These men would have crossed paths many times but particularly when they were both members of the Board of Guardians.

Mr. Wilkes had a pungent manner in expressing himself and an incident to illustrate this was recounted by Reuben Farley himself, *"I remember attending one of Mr. Willmore's Sunday services in the dining room of the new Workhouse when it appeared very manifest that the addition of a harmonium would serve materially to improve the quality of the singing. I mentioned the matter to Mr. J.A. Kenrick, the chairman of the Board and he proposed a resolution for the purchase of a suitable harmonium. Immediately it was seconded Mr. Wilkes sprang to his feet and said, 'I move Mr. Chairman that we engage a dancing master for the paupers'. This prompted a good deal of laughter and the proposal to buy a harmonium was defeated – but within a few weeks Mr. Kenrick had provided one at his own cost."*

This behaviour was typical of Wilkes who opposed spending money on unnecessary 'frills' although no one was more ready to give an old man a pair of shoes or a widow an extra loaf than he.

Blunt and outspoken he championed the cause of the poor and oppressed. He gained a reputation as an upholder of the rights of the common people, a zealous fighter against the waste of ratepayers money or of any other cause he believed in, a zeal that would get him into trouble and even land him in prison but this only served to make him more popular. Over the years he became an almost legendary character.

He grew up in the rural district of Wigmore and was described as a ruddy complexioned mischievous boy who at 15 already displayed the characteristics that became so pronounced in later years. He and his brother took an axe and saw to level a fence which had been erected to block a footpath across the fields.

He evidently prospered in business as a barber at Mayers Green and built himself a house close by in Virgins End (later to become 47 Reform Street). At that time it was a green and pleasant place looking out over the open heath. As a hairdresser in those days he would regularly attend customers in their own homes. Twice a day he would leave his establishment on his professional rounds carrying on his arm a basket containing the implements of his business and with the shaving can hanging from one of his fingers. He became a familiar figure in the town and had a large circle of customers and acquaintances.

At the passing of the Reform Act in 1832 he came out as an energetic and enthusiastic leader of the popular movement in the parish. He and his friends discussed literature of the Reform Party at his house and he had the word Reform painted over his doorway. Although not a formal one, a Reform Club came into existence and he became the leader of reform agitation in the town. This is why the area where he lived became Reform Street.

He took a leading part in the movement to secure the appointment of a Board of Commissioners to govern the town. He and his supporters pursued a campaign against workhouse mismanagement which led on one occasion to the offending governor being removed but perhaps the incident for which he is best remembered was his successful resistance to the proposed closing of Lyne Pearl Well in 1848. The preservation for public use of that ancient spring won for him the gratitude of the residents of Lyndon who relied upon it for their water supply and had an unshakeable belief in its crystal purity.

In 1867 a proposal was made to erect a public drinking fountain in Dartmouth Square as a memento of the services "Barber" Wilkes had rendered to the community but it was not taken any further. It was left to Alderman Farley to give practical effect to the same idea eighteen years later when he placed a fountain there in memory of his mother a few months after her death.

Also in 1867 an alteration was made in the law governing the qualification to hold the office of a Guardian of the Poor. The new enactment provided that a person to be a Guardian must be rated in respect of property of an annual rental of £25 and must personally pay the poor rate which was usually paid by the landlord and charged by him as part of the rent. Four members of the West Bromwich Board – Mr. Wilkes, Mr. Hampton, Mr. Brough and Mr. Horton – ceased to be eligible and their membership terminated with expiry of the term of the Board of 1867-68. Although he admitted there were a few honest men among the Guardians, Mr. Wilkes dramatically 'washed his hands' of the Board at their meeting on March 31st, 1868.

After some fourteen years as a member of the Board of Guardians his tenure of office came to an end.

By the end of the century Reuben Farley, the first freeman of West Bromwich and close ally of the fifth and sixth Earls of Dartmouth, replaced Wilkes as the town's most popular citizen.

Note:
The Boardroom building of the Workhouse Guardians still stands on Hallam Street today. A blue plaque erected by the Pauper Memorial Committee and West Bromwich Local History Society marks the location where the Guardians of the Poor ran their business for the Hallam House Workhouse from 1857 to 1930.

WEST BROMWICH TOWN HALL

In the beginning there was the land, owned by the rich Izon family but previously part of the West Bromwich Heath before the 1804 Enclosure Act. This prime land, known as the Lodge Estate, was purchased from Messrs. John York and others acting as Trustees of William Izon deceased, 'for the erection of a complex of public buildings including a town hall designed to provide accommodation for the civic business in the town; to enhance the prestige of its dignitaries and also improve the social life of the town's population in general.'

The need for new buildings was recorded by F.W. Hackwood the noted Black Country historian, in his book *A History of West Bromwich*.

'By this date (1854) there were in existence some churches and chapels; but these were the only class of public buildings to be found within the confines of the parish ... (there was) an absence of public buildings for conducting the Municipal and social life of the community.'

The West Bromwich Improvement Commissioners, between 1854 and 1882, were elected to govern and as such were responsible for the design, planning and erection of these public buildings. The Improvement Commissioners decided to advertise a competition for architects to submit designs for these public buildings which included a town hall. *The Building News, 27 October 1871* states that: 'Twenty-nine architects submitted plans for the buildings for the consideration of the Improvement Commissioners.'

In their wisdom, and due to their lack of knowledge in architectural matters, the Town Commissioners appointed an eminent London architect, Ewan Christian, who worked for the Ecclesiastical Commissioners, to examine and give his opinion upon all the plans sent in for the proposed public buildings. As a result of Christian's detailed report and recommendations the design of architects

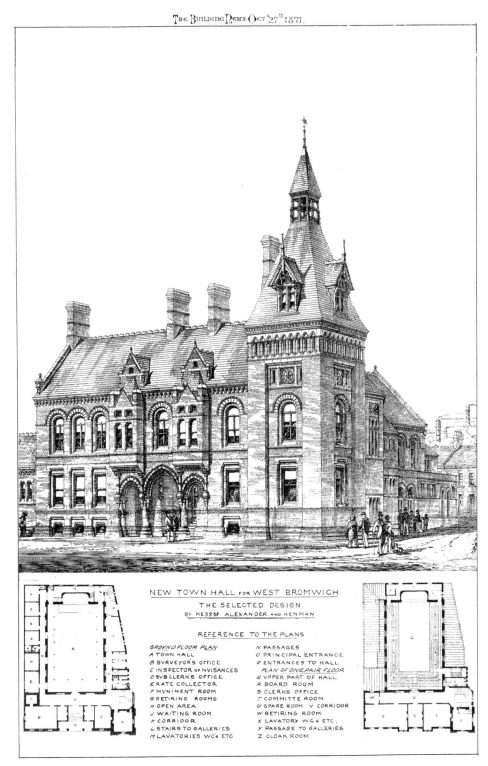

The Building News Oct 27, 1871.

Alexander & Henman, Stockton-on-Tees, Middlesbrough, was accepted for the Town Hall. A sum of £240 was given to the successful competitors.

By November 1871 the Town Commissioners had received tenders for the erection of the building from various contractors. Messrs. Trow & Son, Wednesbury, was given the contract to erect a town hall having submitted the lowest tender. The members of the Committee stated that, 'As the cost of the building is limited it has been necessary to use materials of an inexpensive description to keep the design as simple as is compatible with a certain character required in a Public Building'.

In October 1872 the Town Improvement Commissioners resolved to use common bricks at the back and side of the Town Hall instead of dressed bricks 'whereby savings were affected'. Earlier that year as result of studying a report from architects that there would be a space between the hall and Lodge Road which would need to be fenced off, the Commissioners decided to pay an additional £75 to use that space as additional internal accommodation, when it was considered that by that course a considerable outlay for fencing will be saved. But the Commissioners refused the architects' suggestion that the lighting in the retiring rooms should be from the side walls instead of the roof.

The Improvement Commissioners Minutes, dated May 14, 1873 record: 'Your Committee have further considered the proposed designs of the architects for heightening the tower of the Town Hall 15 feet and giving an additional room at a cost of about £270 and unanimously resolved to recommend to your Board to carry out the alteration which will add greatly to improve the effect of the whole building'.

The West Bromwich News, dated 14 August 1875, gives the following detailed description of the exterior of this building. "Noticing the Town Hall, it must at the outset be admitted that the place is one which in every sense of the word is a credit to the town. It is an architectural triumph of which the people of West Bromwich need justly be proud. The hall, which stands out prominently as the visitor enters the place either from the north or south sides of the district, stands on the corner site of the Lodge Estate and has a frontage to the main road of about 130 feet. Externally the design is of bold proportions, having at the outer corner a massive tower rising to a height of over 130 feet, the upper stage being ornamented with a continuous arcade of detached columns and trefoils arches with a richly moulded cornice above, under the curves of a high pitched roof broken up by large dormer windows and a handsome group of chimneys on one side. From the front dormer is supported a lofty flagstaff. The tower stands slightly forward and forms a very picturesque object, and can be seen a long distance off.

"Below the arcading and around the tower circular openings are designed to receive an illuminated clock; but as yet nothing has been mooted with regard to the purchase of the great enemy's pace. Above the two side arches of the entrance, corbelled out from the wall are bay windows with ornamental gablets which pleasantly break up the main roof. The windows generally to the basement and ground floor have moulded stone lintels and those of the first floor semi-circular arched heads of brick and terracotta carving having an ornamental hood mould of the latest material of which also the string courses, the cornices, arcading to tower etc. are made. Red pressed bricks are employed for the general facings and green slates with red tile castings form the covering of the roofs."

All records show that the Town Hall was built in brick and stone in an Italian Gothic style and was erected 1874-1875. It was altered in 1905 to provide more offices and a Committee Room. In 1924 the Reading Room of the former Free Library building, next to the Town Hall was converted into a Council Chamber.

At long last the scene was set for the inhabitants of the town to celebrate the completion of this "architectural triumph", which was officially handed over to the Town's Improvement Commissioners. It was decided that the Town Hall would be formally opened on 10 August 1875. *"Mr. Reuben Farley, Chairman of the Commissioners, generously decided to mark this auspicious occasion with a Banquet, to be held in the new prestigious Town Hall. Invitations were issued to 'most of the public bodies in the town, including the gentlemen who gave their time and attention to public duties'." (West Bromwich Weekly News, 1875.)*

The Chairman did not forget the ladies and invitations were issued to them for coffee at six o'clock, and from the galleries they had the privilege of viewing the "lords of creation" and listening to the speeches.

With everything in place the Board of Commissioners and their illustrious guests prepared to enjoy and celebrate the completion of the long-awaited fruits of their labours with the proposed banquet which the local newspaper described in detail.

'A large and fashionable company assembled at six o'clock, when the road immediately between Christ Church to the Public Buildings was literally blocked with spectators, who all seemed anxious to catch a glimpse of the personages who alighted from their carriages in front of the Town Hall. A small body of police was on the spot, who effectively prevented any possible disorder or indecorum. Early in the morning the bells of Christ Church were ringing and the national flag was hoisted on the tower of the hall.

'The fine spacious hall was appropriately decorated; the orchestra which was occupied by Messrs. Synyer and Gilmer's band, assuming a pretty appearance. During the evening the band enlivened the proceedings by giving in the most artistic manner, a selection of operatic music.'

The 'sumptuous banquet' lasted about two hours and there followed the inevitable speeches, responses and toasts to the Queen; the Earl of Dartmouth and all honoured guests. A well deserved speech of thanks and a toast was made to 'The Chairman' who in response said,

"As a native of West Bromwich he had striven, and should still strive, to the end of his days to do what he could towards the advancement of the town, (loud applause). He would again thank them heartily for the honour which they had done him."

Seven years later, in 1882, another banquet was held in the Town Hall to celebrate the town being given the status of a Municipal Borough by being granted a Charter of Incorporation. This memorable achievement was acknowledged in the General Purposes Committee Report of the Town Council, 'Your Committee have resolved to have the front of the Public Buildings illuminated on the occasion of the Banquet given by the Mayor, to celebrate the Incorporation of the Borough, on the 7th proximo'.

On the High Street the illumination of the municipal buildings was a most elaborate scale – probably seeming all the more spectacular as pre-event snowfall and cold wind almost ruined the atmosphere of anticipation inside and outside the Town Hall. And inside it was an occasion when the full splendour and richness of the Civic Regalia were in evidence to enhance what was described as a 'brilliant' gathering.

The Mayor (Alderman Reuben Farley) wore the Chain of Office presented by the Earl of Dartmouth for the first time and the Silver Mace, given to the Borough by the Mayor, occupied a place worthy of its magnificence on the table in front of him. A formal presentation of the Chain of Office and the Silver Mace was made to the Mayor and Corporation at a later date.

For many years to come the Town Hall would have an important place in the life of the town. Apart from the official function of municipal administration the building would be the venue for all sorts of social events – concerts, dances, bazaars, Remembrance Day Services and school speech days. These events have been described in, as with much of the above text taken from the award winning book, *West Bromwich Town Hall,* published in 2003 by the West Bromwich Library User Group. The outside of the building would provide the backdrop for official proclamations and the celebration of Albion's football triumphs. Architectural historian, Nikolaus Pevsner, in his monumental series, *The Buildings of England,* would give the Town Hall recognition not only for its Gothic symmetry but lack of High Victorian assertiveness. Thirteen years after his slightly grudging remarks English Heritage made an assessment regarding the importance of the Town Hall as part of the heritage of West Bromwich with the result that it was granted the status of a Grade II Listed Building.

CHAPTER FOUR

Farley In His Own Words

FARLEY IN HIS OWN WORDS;
SOME PERSONAL REMINISCENCES

'In promising to write an article upon the Rise and Progress in West Bromwich during our good Queen's reign of sixty years, I am afraid my good nature ran away with my judgement. The more I think about the subject the greater and more difficult it appears to compress within the limits of a newspaper article. However, as I have promised I must do my best under the circumstances.'

Queen Victoria's Diamond Jubilee was celebrated in 1897 when the *Free Press* published a series of articles, written by Reuben Farley, in which he reflected upon the 'Rise and Progress of West Bromwich in the Queen's Reign'. Great changes came about in society following on the success of the Industrial Revolution in which the Black Country played a leading role. As West Bromwich turned from a sparsely populated area into a prosperous town new institutions and services were required and Farley's writings show how he and others responded to these challenges.

EDUCATION

In his first main topic Farley reflected in part on his own education as a child and later in the provision of technical education and the acquisition of knowledge as a social enjoyment.

Sixty years ago there were no Board Schools, and to give a child such an education that he now receives gratis would have cost a small fortune. There was a British and National School near All Saints' Church, and the Earl of Dartmouth (the present Earl's grandfather) paid for the education of a number of poor boys, also providing them with clothing – green jackets and corduroy breeches. There were a few Dame and private adventure schools, where the children of poor parents were taught reading and writing with a little arithmetic with fees varying from threepence to tenpence per week. The three principal schools were Borwick Heath House Academy, Skilly's School, near the old Parish Church, and Marshall's School at Hill Top. At Mr. Borwick's School there were about 10 boarders and 30 day scholars. Alderman Rollason was a boarder and I was a day scholar. The ordinary fees for day scholars were six guineas per annum which included Latin and Greek, drawing four guineas per annum; French, music and dancing were also extras.

Jacquis's boys were known in the parish as my lord's scholars, but as there was an old feud between Borwick's and Jacquis's boys these charity boys were dubbed, "Jacquis's bull dogs". It was considered good form to make up a party to go out of bounds to attack Jacquis's boys and it was my lot to be in more than one of the scrimmages. Upon one memorable occasion Borwick's boys came off second best – a black eye and a torn jacket fell to my portion.

There was a small mechanics institution at the Swan Village Gas Works, conducted by the manager of the gasworks which had only a short existence. This was followed by the establishment of the West Bromwich institution for the advancement of knowledge, in a house now in the occupation of Cooper and Son, in High Street, opposite Wesley Chapel. For 40 years, or thereabouts, this institution served a useful purpose to those members who availed themselves of its advantages. There was a circulating library of about 600 volumes, a reading room and classes for mathematics, French, shorthand and debating. When I was 18 years of age I became a member, and was very soon appointed assistant honorary secretary, which gave me a taste for public work. What rapid strides education has made during the Queen's reign. In the year 1867 Earl Russell moved a resolution in the House of Lords asserting the principle "that every child has the right to education." Then came the Elementary Education Bill of Mr. W.E. Forster, which received the Royal Assent on the 9th August 1870. A public meeting was held in St. George's Hall, Paradise Street, now in the occupation of Mr. A.A. James, when a resolution was passed to establish a School Board.

After the accession of the Queen, and long before the passing of the Education Act of 1870 – the exact dates I have not been able to ascertain – several large employers of labour, recognising the value and importance of elementary education, established schools for the children of their workpeople. Notably, Messrs. Archibald Kenrick and Sons, Messrs. Chance Brothers and Co., and Messrs. John Bagnall and Sons. It was not a hard and fast line to limit their privileges to the children of their own workpeople, as other children were eligible, so far as accommodation could be found. There are no accurate statistics of the number of boys and girls at day schools when Victoria became Queen of England. In all probability that number did not exceed 1,000. Contrast the condition of education then with what it is now! At the present time the number of scholars on the books of our Board Schools is 7,438, denominational schools is 5,318, private adventure schools estimated at 316; making a total of 13,072; all being taught by efficient trained masters and mistresses, and this number large as it is , does not include the children at Wigmore School.

When I visited the inmates of the Workhouse, I was struck with the dull, heavy and sullen appearance of the children in the Workhouse, so different to the bright and cheerful appearance of the boys and girls in some denominational schools where I was at that time a manager. In pondering over these matters I arrived at the conclusion that if the boys and girls at the Union Workhouse, some of whom were orphans, were to be raised from pauperism and given a fair chance in life, it was of paramount importance that they should be removed from the taint of their surroundings. It is a truism, that surroundings have a great influence upon everybody, either for good or for evil. Very unsatisfactory reports had been received of those boys and girls who had been placed out in situations. At a convenient opportunity I brought this important question before the Board, when I had the satisfaction to find that my suggestion for the removal of the children from the Workhouse to a separate school building met with the approval of the more intelligent Guardians, who were present on that occasion. The outcome of that morning's discussion, in process of time, was the establishment of the Wigmore District Schools, which were opened in May 1872. These schools are doing good work. There is a marked contrast in the appearance of both boys and girls, who now present a bright and happy appearance. There is a smartness about the boys in the Band, which is a credit to the managers and all concerned.

In the autumn of 1881 Mr. Fred Ryland consulted me about the establishment of an Institute in West Bromwich on similar lines to the Midland Institute, Birmingham, having for its object, higher education, technical instruction, and social enjoyment. A preliminary meeting of manufacturers and educationists was held at the School Board Offices in October, 1881, when Mr. Ryland's project met with a favourable reception. On 27th February, 1882, a public meeting was held in the Town Hall, the Earl of Dartmouth in the chair, when resolutions of approval were passed, and a committee appointed to bring the project to a successful issue. At the first meeting of the committee, I was elected chairman, Mr. Fred Ryland hon. secretary, and Mr. John H. Chance treasurer. The foundation stone was laid on 4th August 1884, in glorious weather and amid great rejoicing. The Institute was opened on the 6th. May1886, when the Mayor (Alderman Rollason) gave a conversazione to celebrate the event.

The Council of the Institute managed the Science and Art Schools until 1st January, 1891, when the Town Council adopted the schools as Municipal Schools. It would be difficult to exaggerate the value and importance of these schools to the industrial, commercial, and social life of West Bromwich. The Art School especially has taken high rank among the Art Schools of England, thanks to the teaching ability and culture of the head master, Mr. Pearce. At the present time there are 488 students in the Art School; 270 in the Science School; 252 in the Branch Schools, 83 in the School of Music, making a grand total 1,093 students. When the building was transferred to the Corporation, the news room and lecture theatre were reserved for the use of members of the Institute. The lectures and entertainments provided are always of a high class character, and it is a source of regret that a larger number do not avail themselves of the privileges of the Institute. The number of members on the books is about 360. It gives me pleasure to bear testimony to the excellent work Mr. Ryland has done for the Institute and for the promotion of Technical instruction in West Bromwich; and it would not be fair to leave out the names of Mr. George Salter, Dr. Underhill, Mr. Kenneth Macauley, and Mr. William Bache, all of whom have rendered most valuable assistance.

HEALTH AND WELFARE

What today we term social issues were his next big projects to be addressed as during Queen Victoria's reign the population of West Bromwich increased more than threefold.

Somewhere about the year 1864 the Provident Medical Dispensary was born. A room was rented in the house, now in the occupation of Bullus and Co., chemists in High Street. This Dispensary was a combination of charity and provident contributions. Mr. John Manley and Mr. Kite were medical officers, receiving remuneration for their services. There was a small committee of management, and when I became a member Mr. J.A. Kenrick was the chairman, and Mr. P.D. Bennett hon. secretary. At one of the committee meetings there was an interesting conversation about hospitals. It was felt that West Bromwich as a mining and manufacturing town ought to have a hospital. Cases were cited of injured men dying on their way to the Birmingham Hospitals. The outcome of this conversation was the desire to found a hospital for the benefit of the town and surrounding district. Dr. Silvester's house, the present residence of Mr. Enoch Wood, to whom it belongs, was then void, and several members of the committee wanted that house to be bought and converted into a hospital. Happily, the majority were in favour of buying a clean piece of land, and so building a good modern hospital. The foundation stone was laid by the Countess of Dartmouth (now Dowager Countess) on the 21st September, 1869, and opened for the reception of patients early in 1871.

The money outlay upon the land and buildings was £9,000, raised by voluntary contributions. The first chairman was Mr. John Arthur Kenrick; Mr. P.D. Bennett, hon. secretary and Major Williams, treasurer. The hon. medical staff consisted of Mr. Henry Sutcliffe, Mr. Thomas Sansome, and Mr. H. Langley Browne. At the commencement there was some adverse criticism upon the youth of our medical staff. That cannot apply in this year of grace: but there has never been any want of confidence in their skill and ability. A new wing was added in 1881 at a cost of £3,500, and more recently there is the important extension of two circular wards at a further outlay of £8,000. Adequate provision has now been made for the Eye Department, which has so much increased the usefulness of this beneficent institution. The Outpatients Department was erected by the present Chairman of the Board of Management, Mr. John Homer Chance, at his own cost. Mr. William Bache is the hon. secretary, and Mr. Fred Ryland treasurer. There was a grand total of 10,968 patients from West Bromwich, Wednesbury, Oldbury, and West Smethwick, who received the benefit of this noble institution last year. The income for the support of the Hospital is derived from several sources. Annual subscribers, Hospital Sunday and Sunday School scholars collections, interest which accrues from a small endowment fund, and last, though not least, the Hospital Saturday collections. At the commencement of this year there was a debt of £2,000 upon the new building account of the Circular Wards. It is anticipated that this incubus of debt will be extinguished before the close of this Diamond Jubilee year.

The West Bromwich Building Permanent Society was established in the year 1849 on a modest scale, with only 25 members. At the present time the society contains 2,480 members. Mr. John Silvester was the first president. In 1864 I was elected president and I have filled the office ever since. Mr. J.P. Sharpe was the first secretary and Mr. John Hampton was elected as his successor, and he had filled the office ever since. During the existence of this Society, it has encouraged and promoted habits of thrift among the people, and by its agency large numbers have been enabled to become the owners of house property, and thereby to make some provision against the time of sickness and old age, and for those dependent upon them by the ties of nature and kindred.

Although Farley had not mentioned in his articles he had in 1878 called for greater fire safety and for the establishment of a proper fire brigade. For the brigade's annual dinner he personally contributed the highest subscription to the prize fund.

Sixty years ago there was a Manual Fire Engine located in New Street, belonging to and maintained by the Lancashire Fire Insurance Company. After the death of Mr. William Salter the fire engine was removed to the rear of Mr. William Burch's house, adjoining Hudson's Passage. At one time, Mr. Thomas Friend, with some neighbouring shopkeepers, formed a Volunteer Brigade with a small manual engine. This brigade lived a few years. At the end of the year 1880, or thereabouts, a serious fire broke out in Digbeth, Birmingham, which caused a serious loss of life. This calamity created a painful impression in Birmingham and South Staffordshire. At West Bromwich early in 1881 the Commissioners decided to establish a Volunteer Fire Brigade for the protection of life and property. The Volunteer Brigade comprised of 10 men all told, with Mr. W.H. Wayte as Captain. A small steam fire engine was provided, capacity 359 gallons per minute, also 900 feet of hose. At first the brigade was called together by the primitive method of ringing an alarm bell, fixed at the top of the Fire Station, which was more effectual at getting a crowd together than calling up the firemen. The first fire this newly formed Brigade was called out to was at Wilke's Foundry in Oldbury. At a Town Council meeting held in May 1883 it was resolved to make the brigade more reliable by paying the men for their services. Recognising the responsibility for providing adequate means for the protection of life and property, the Town Council has, from time to time, made important additions and improvements. At the present time we have a steam fire engine capable of pumping 600 gallons of water per minute; a smaller one for 350 gallons, tender with complete equipment for hose, life saving apparatus, ambulance dressings, &c, one 5½ feet fire escape, electric apparatus for calling up all the firemen, as well as the horses, 2 substations, 4 street fire alarms, 420 fire hydrants, and the Fire Station is kept open all day and night continuously. The brigade consists now of 20 men all told, with Captain Wayte as Chief Officer. A shrewd critic once remarked, if you want to find out whether a town is well governed, pay a visit to the Fire Station. Judged by that test, of a truth West Bromwich would come out well, and stand favourable comparison with any English town of equal size and population.

GAS: A FIGHT WITH THE NEIGHBOURS

In lesson for today's energy supply the Town Commissioners looked for the advantages in public control with an element of profit. Securing a gas supply for West Bromwich was one of Farley's big fights and in itself an achievement.

When it became known that Birmingham had entered into an agreement, subject to the consent of Parliament, to purchase the undertaking of the Birmingham and Staffordshire Gas Light and Coal Company, we tried, by friendly negotiation, to obtain the insertion of a Clause in the proposed Birmingham Gas Bill, to give West Bromwich and other outside authorities the right to purchase on the same basis, their respective portions of the gas undertaking. As we did not succeed we petitioned Parliament against the bill. The House of Commons Committee declared the preamble of the Bill to be proved. Our Counsel then advised us not to oppose the clauses before that committee but reserve our opposition for the House of Lords Committee. The advice was sound and we succeeded in getting a purchasing clause inserted in the Birmingham Gas Bill. We had several good gas engineering witnesses, and I was the only other witness called for the outside authorities. Birmingham gained its Gas Bill in 1875, West Bromwich in the next session 1876. The prices to be paid to Birmingham had to be settled by arbitration. Mr. Hawkesley acted as arbitrator for Birmingham, Mr. Bramwell for West Bromwich. Sir Henry Hunt was the umpire. Mr. John Field gave some valuable mining evidence on behalf of the Commissioners. Mr. Charles Bayley prepared the Commissioners' case with marked ability. The sittings were held in George Street, Westminster, and dragged their slow length along for 24 days. When I remonstrated with Counsel about the length of the proceedings, I was assured that it was a most interesting and important arbitration which should not be hurried. As those gentlemen were earning handsome fees day by day, and as I was there all the time as a witness and to watch the proceedings, at great inconvenience and loss, as I paid my own expenses, they evidently regarded the matter from a different standpoint to what I did. However, all's well that ends well. When the award came we were satisfied. Birmingham claimed for the gas mains, meters and good will £180,000. West Bromwich wanted to buy for £60,000. The award was £70,750. Birmingham appealed against the award, both in the Courts of Queen's Bench and before the Lords Justices of Appeal. In both Courts the appeal was dismissed with costs. As we were only purchasing the distributing apparatus, with the right to supply the whole parish of West Bromwich, we had to build manufacturing works. A good site was secured near the Albion Railway Station, having both railway and canal facilities of transit upon which good modern gasworks have been erected. The purchase money was paid over to the Corporation of Birmingham on the 1st July 1880 and on that day I had the pleasure of turning on the gas from the Albion Gasworks, in the presence of my colleagues. A few figures will show some of the advantages which have accrued to our borough from the gas undertaking. Out of gas profits £29,000 has been set aside for the redemption of capital outlay, £4,000 to a depreciation fund, £20,000 to the relief of the rates, and £11,690 for working capital. There is also this further advantage; an important town like West Bromwich is not dependent upon an outside town for its supply of gas. When the capital outlay is extinguished, if the earning power of the gas undertaking is then no better than what it is at the present time, the Gas Committee will be in a position to transfer out of profits £5,000 per annum in aid of the rates.

PARKS FOR THE PEOPLE

When I read in the Birmingham newspaper that Miss Ryland had presented to Birmingham Cannon Hill Park, the idea occurred to me what a good thing it would be for West Bromwich if the late Earl of Dartmouth could be induced to give a slice of Sandwell Park for a public park. I wrote to Lord Dartmouth and received an invitation to go to Patshull. To the best of my ability I laid the case before the noble lord, how great a boon he would confer upon his native town if he would give to the Commissioners fifty acres of land for the purpose of a public park. He said that he would think the matter over and as it was entailed property he would have to consult his son, Viscount Lewisham. In a short time I received an invitation to dine with Lord Dartmouth at the Rifle Volunteers' encampment, Sandwell Park. After luncheon we adjourned with Lord Lewisham to Lord Dartmouth's tent, and over cigars and coffee we further discussed this grant of land. After a most friendly conversation he said to his son in a cheerful way, "Now Lewisham, what do you say? Mr. Farley must have an answer." Lord Lewisham replied promptly, "Yes, I am agreeable but he must not come this thing too often." By appointment soon afterwards I met a surveyor from Messrs. Thynne's Office at Coopers Hill who brought a plan of Sandwell Park, upon which I was allowed to mark out in pencil the proposed Public Park. The surveyor said that his instructions were not to be to an acre or two. I was not altogether inexperienced with plans, but when I scaled the portion I had marked out I was rather disconcerted to discover it measured up to 56 acres. And that quantity the Earl of Dartmouth and his son generously agreed to. The land was enclosed and laid out by the Improvement Commissioners and out of compliment to the generous donors it was christened Dartmouth Park. Upon a gala day, never to be forgotten in West Bromwich, Monday, the 3rd June 1878, the park was opened and dedicated to the public for their free use and enjoyment, by that right honourable and worthy nobleman, the late Earl of Dartmouth. At night there was a grand display of fireworks to celebrate the event.

Early in November 1886 I approached the Earl again for an additional piece of land to be added to the Park for the purpose of making boating and bathing pools, and at the meeting of our Town Council held on 5th January 1887, I had the pleasure and satisfaction to move – "That the best and grateful thanks of this Council be presented to the Right Honourable, the Earl of Dartmouth for the proposed addition to the Park of a piece of land containing 9 acres, 1 rood and 17 perches." The first sod of this desirable extension was cut by the noble donor on the Saturday in Jubilee Week, 1887. Dartmouth Park now contains 65 acres of fine, undulating land, well timbered and tastefully laid out and on the whole is the finest Public Park in the Midland Counties.

Sometimes, when I am walking through the Park on a Sunday with our Park Keeper, Mr. Henry Browne, my heart overflows with gratitude to the Great Giver of all Good that he ever put it into the heart of Lord Dartmouth to confer this priceless boon upon the inhabitants of West Bromwich.

Although the acquisition of Dartmouth Park was highly appreciated, and continued to grow in public favour and usefulness, there were murmurings from time to time in the Town Council, from representatives from Hill Top and Greets Green Wards. These two wards are furthest removed from Dartmouth Park, so that while the burgesses of those wards were called upon to contribute prorata with the burgesses of other wards, from their geographical position they were precluded from enjoying equal advantages. Jubilee year, 1887, presented a favourable opportunity for bringing under the notice of landed proprietors the many blessings they had enjoyed under the Queen's reign of 60 years, blessings which are deserving of a recognition of duties and responsibilities.

In Greets Green Ward there was a detached part of the Whitehall Estate having a frontage to Whitehall Road, altogether suitable for a public recreation ground. The owner, Mr. Jones, lived at Lee in Kent. As there is nothing like a personal interview in matters of this kind, I obtained an appointment and saw Mr. Jones at his house. The interview was very pleasant, his grandfather having been a personal friend of my father, and he expressed regret that he could not afford to give the land for so good an object. Then I asked him if he would sell it to me, as from old associations I felt a strong interest in Greets Green. For certain reasons, which he gave, he refused to sell, and I came away disappointed.

After some further correspondence, at a subsequent interview Mr. Jones agreed to sell, and on the 6th January 1891, I had the pleasure to offer to the Corporation this land, containing about six acres. It has been skilfully and tastefully laid out, and planted with shrubs and trees. An entrance lodge, with a commodious reading room, has also been provided. The opening day was 1st August, 1892, in Mr. Councillor Salter's year of Mayoralty. It is doing something towards brightening the lives of the children and adults in that part of our Borough; and the inhabitants, headed by Mr. Jonathan Bywater, (who is a tower of strength at Greets Green), have erected a handsome band stand and provided a large number of chairs.

In Jubilee year, 1887, by appointment I went over to Penn to see Mrs. Spittle, who cheerfully promised to give about seven acres of land at Harvilles Hawthorn, in the Hill Top Ward, for a recreation ground. Unfortunately there was a boundary dispute with Great Western Railway Company, and worse still, the situation of the land was not regarded as altogether suitable for the purpose. Mrs. Spittle's generous offer was therefore allowed to glide. On the 5th November 1895 an offer was made through Mr. Councillor Wilson to sell Tyrell House and grounds, containing about six acres, for the very reasonable price of £1,000. As the situation is everything that could be desired and the price was so cheap, the Corporation accepted the offer. The first idea was to alter and adapt Tyrell House for a reading room, police station and caretaker's rooms, but upon further consideration wiser counsels prevailed. The old house has been pulled down. Plans have been prepared by the Borough Surveyor (Mr. Greatordex) and tenders obtained for a new structure to contain all that is required in better form. By erecting the new building nearer to the public road other advantages are gained.

A further important addition to the lungs of West Bromwich will be opened and dedicated to the public on Monday next, 2nd August, by the worthy donors, Messrs. John Arthur and William Kenrick. The Kenrick Park contains about 19 acres. Early next year it is expected that Oak House Museum and pleasure grounds will be opened. West Bromwich is therefore rapidly becoming well provided with open spaces, so conducive to health and longevity. As:

"Man never is but always to be blest."

It remains to be seen whether the burgesses like Oliver Twist, will ask for more.

FROM POORHOUSE AND PARISH TO A PROPER TOWN

At the commencement of the Queen's long and glorious reign and for a period of 20 years afterwards, the West Bromwich Board of Guardians held their meetings in the Club Room at the Dartmouth Hotel. At the election of Guardians in 1852 I was elected a Guardian of the Poor and at the first meeting of the new Board, Mr. Joseph Smith, of Wednesbury was elected chairman in succession to the Rev. Isaacs Clarkson, who refused to continue in that office any longer, Mr. Charles Stringer acted as Clerk. The old Workhouse, sometimes called the Poor House, was situated in Lyndon, at the back of the old Horse and Jockey Inn. A nail warehouse which at one time belonged to Mr. Turton, had been altered and adapted for the purpose, and was only capable of providing accommodation for about 60 inmates. There was also an old Workhouse at Wednesbury. It was found impossible to apply the House test even to able bodied applicants for relief. Moreover, the Poor Law Board was pressing the Guardians from time to time, to build a proper Union Workhouse. Some timid members of the Board were alarmed at the prospect of embarking on such a big undertaking. The idea, of borrowing so large a sum upon the security of the rates, frightened them. As time went on however, the necessity of the case became far more urgent, and it was at length resolved to purchase the necessary land, and so comply with the wishes of the Poor Law Board. The purchase of the land was completed in March 1856. Inmates were received into the new Workhouse building somewhere about September 1857 and I am under the impression that the first Board meeting was held in the Board Room at the Union Workhouse in the following month. There were two candidates for the office of Chaplain to the new Union Workhouse, the Rev. Benjamin Willmore, Trinity Parsonage, and the Rev. Isaac Bickerstaff, curate in charge at All Saints. As the new Union Workhouse was in All Saints parish, and as the Rev. Isaac Bickerstaff had been the most diligent in his ministrations to the inmates of the old Workhouse without receiving any stipend, in my innocence I made sure that Mr. Bickerstaff would receive the appointment. To my surprise Mr. Willmore obtained the majority of votes, and was therefore duly elected Chaplain. I remember attending one of Mr. Willmore's Sunday Services in the Dining Room of the new Workhouse, very soon after his appointment, when it appeared very manifest that the addition of a harmonium would serve to materially improve the quality of the singing. From enquiries it appeared there would be no difficulty in obtaining the services of a competent person to officiate at such an instrument without occurring any extra expense. As Mr. J.A. Kenrick was at that time chairman of the Board, I mentioned the matter to him, and he proposed a resolution for the purchase of a suitable harmonium. Immediately it was seconded, Mr. Wilkes, (better known as Barber Wilkes) sprang to his feet and said, "I move Mr. Chairman that we engage a dancing master for them 'ere paupers." This sally provoked a great deal of laughter and I am sorry to have occasion to record the fact that to buy an instrument at the cost of the rates was thus defeated. Mr. Kenrick whispered to me that a harmonium would be provided, and within a few weeks, at his own cost, there was one delivered by Mr. Samuel Adams. For a period of twenty five years, when the Guardians provided a new harmonium, it blended with the voices of those poor old people in singing praises to that God from whom all blessings flow.

The new Infirmary was opened by the Bishop of Lichfield on 18th December 1884 and the new Board Room, Committee Rooms and Offices were completed November 18th 1887. The present Chairman of the Board is Mr. A.L. Wells, and Mr. Henry Ward has filled the office of Clerk from February 1886. The number of inmates at the present time in the Union Workhouse is 685. On 1st January 1895 the number was 864.

In 1837 West Bromwich was governed by the Parish Vestry and Surveyors of Highways. The guardians of the public peace were the Parish Constables. That bone of contention in those days, Church rates, created some lively Vestry meetings. Mr. George Wilkes, commonly called barber Wilkes, was a keen opponent of Church rates. At one Vestry meeting he complained about the burial fees being too high. The Vicar, the Rev. James Spry, retorted by saying that he should be only too happy to bury Mr. Wilkes for nothing.

The West Bromwich Improvement Act was obtained in 1854, when the government of the town passed out of the hands of the Parish Vestry and Surveyors of Highways into the hands of the 16 Improvement Commissioners. Thirteen members had to be elected, and three County Magistrates were appointed by the Stafford Quarter sessions. With the exception of providing a good Cemetery containing sixteen acres of land, making certain street improvements, improving the sanitation of the Borough, and appointing an Inspector of Nuisances – also a Medical Officer of Health, there was not much anything done for about 18 or 19 years from passing the West Bromwich Improvement Act. To the best of my recollection, Mr. P.B. Bennett was elected Chairman of the Commissioners in 1872, when he brought forward a scheme for the erection of Public Buildings – viz. A Town Hall, Market Hall Free Library and Public Baths. Mr. Edward Caddick and I were deputed to negotiate for the Land from Izon's Trustees, and I think we were successful in making a good bargain for the town. Mr. Bennett resigned the Chairmanship owing to the pressure of his other business engagements and on the 3rd October 1874 I was elected Chairman. To celebrate the completion of the Public Buildings I gave a banquet in the Town Hall on 10th August 1875 to the Commissioners, and all who were engaged in public work in West Bromwich.

There were also present Lord Wrottesley, who was at that time the Lord Lieutenant of the County, the Earl of Dartmouth, Mr. Brogden, M.P. for the Borough of Wednesbury, of which West Bromwich then formed a part, Mr. Michael Arthur Bass and Mr. Samuel Charles Allsop, members for East Staffordshire. It was at this banquet that Mr. Brogden promised the Brogden Organ which was opened on the 6th May 1878, and has proved to be so great an acquisition to our Town Hall. The late Mr. Charles Bayley, Clerk to the Commissioners; Mr. John Manley and I were on the Book Buying Committee, and we succeeded in raising by voluntary contributions, £1,600 for the purchase of books for the reference and Circulating Libraries. A considerable number of books were also presented by various donors. It was at a public meeting held in Prince's Rooms that the Free Libraries Act was adopted on the motion of Mr. Duncalfe.

Elizabeth Farley (Reuben's mother).

Eliza Fellows (Harriet's mother).

Reuben Farley.

Harriet Farley (née Fellows).

I

Francis Dashwood Farley fifth child and Clara Helena Fellows Farley, fourth child.

*Reuben Llewelyn Farley second child
(first son).*

Edith Margaret Farley, first child.

*Harriet with her sons. Reuben L (left),
Charles F (middle), Francis D (right).*

*John Dashwood Farley (grandson of Reuben),
Pamela Margaret Sperling (dau of Charles
Finch Farley), Clara Helena Fellows Wood (dau
of Reuben), Richard Dashwood Farley
(grandson of Reuben).*

*The Oak House
Centenary Event.
John Dashwood Farley
(grandson of Reuben),
Oliver James
Dashwood Farley (gg
grandson of Reuben).*

*West Bromwich Local History Society Event June 2014.
Left to right: Terry Price, Anne Wilkins, Dennis Lawley, Rebecca Lawley, Pauline Lawley, Tom
Farley, Gill Farley, Frances Hutchcocks, John Hutchcocks, Belinda Farley, David Brown, Mary
Rose Farley, Carol Hartill, Moreen Wilkes and Brian Wilkes.*

The Farley Freedom Casket.

Tom with the Freedom Scroll.

Ceremonial Keys: Clock Tower, Oak House, Greets Green Park.

Trowel presented to Reuben Farley to lay the foundation stone of
St Philip's Mission Church, West Bromwich, March 1, 1892.

Mayoral Pendant.

West Bromwich Coat of Arms.

Reuben Farley.

Reuben Farley's son, Francis Dashwood Farley.

Reuben Farley's grandson John Dashwood Farley.

Reuben Farley's great grandson Thomas William Dashwood Farley.

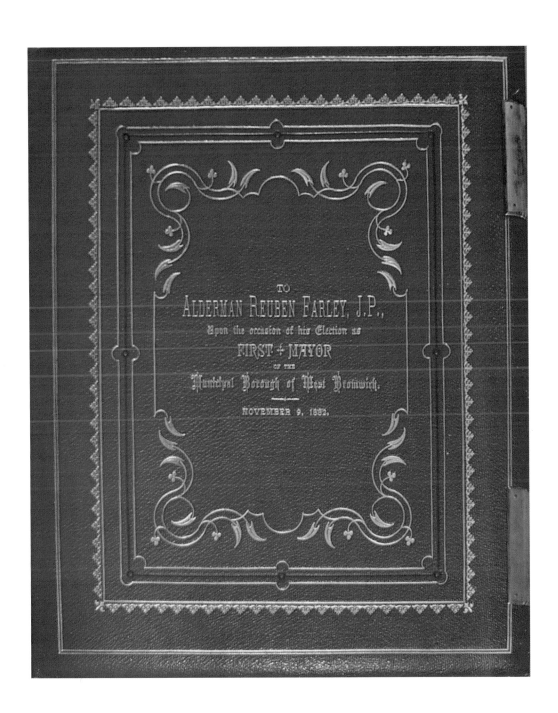

TO
ALDERMAN REUBEN FARLEY, J.P.,
Upon the occasion of his Election as
FIRST ✦ MAYOR
OF THE
Municipal Borough of West Bromwich.

NOVEMBER 9, 1882.

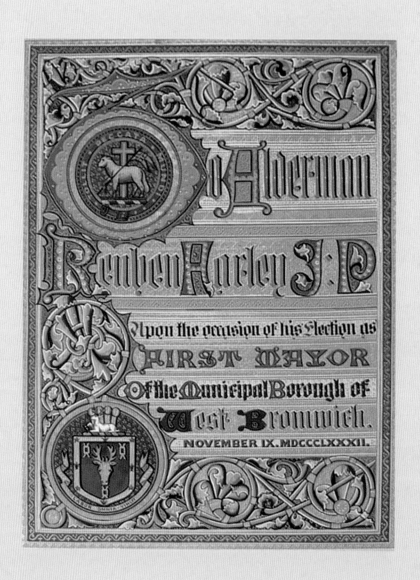

To Alderman

Reuben Farley, J.P.

We the Employés at your Summit Foundry West Bromwich desire to offer to you our hearty

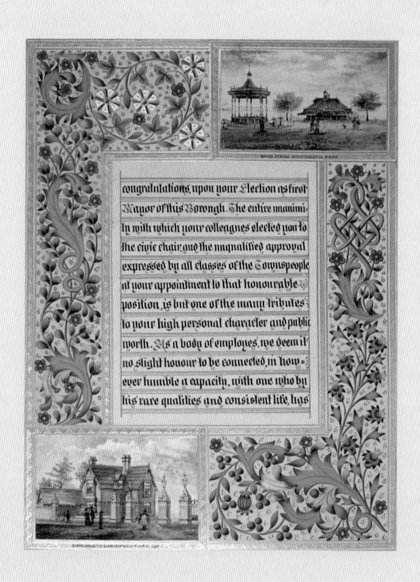

congratulations upon your Election as first Mayor of this Borough. The entire unanimity with which your colleagues elected you to the civic chair, and the unqualified approval expressed by all classes of the Townspeople at your appointment to that honourable position, is but one of the many tributes to your high personal character and public worth. As a body of employés, we deem it no slight honour to be connected in however humble a capacity, with one who by his rare qualities and consistent life, has

justly gained such high distinction amongst
his fellow men.

The honour in which your name is
held is not the glare of a brief popularity, but
is the result of years of labour and love in
the interests of your native Town. From
your earliest manhood you have, in a
marked degree, been identified with all the
principal movements, having for their object the progress and wellbeing of the Town
and its Inhabitants. On all your undertakings, whether as Chairman of the Guardians

THE PUBLIC BATHS

THE HOSPITAL

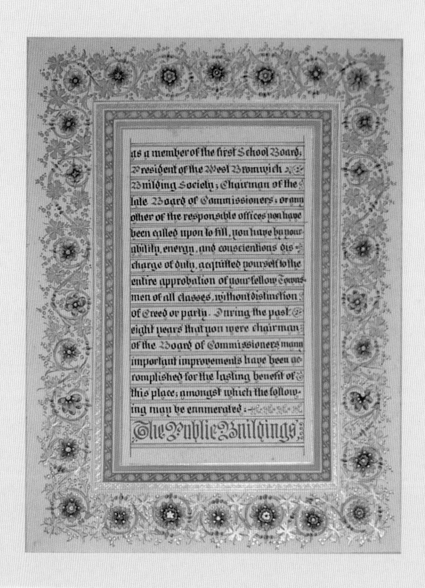

as a member of the first School Board, President of the West Bromwich Building Society, Chairman of the late Board of Commissioners, or any other of the responsible offices you have been called upon to fill, you have by your ability, energy, and conscientious discharge of duty, acquitted yourself to the entire approbation of your fellow Townsmen of all classes, without distinction of Creed or party. During the past eight years that you were chairman of the Board of Commissioners many important improvements have been accomplished for the lasting benefit of this place; amongst which the following may be enumerated :—

The Public Buildings.

XII

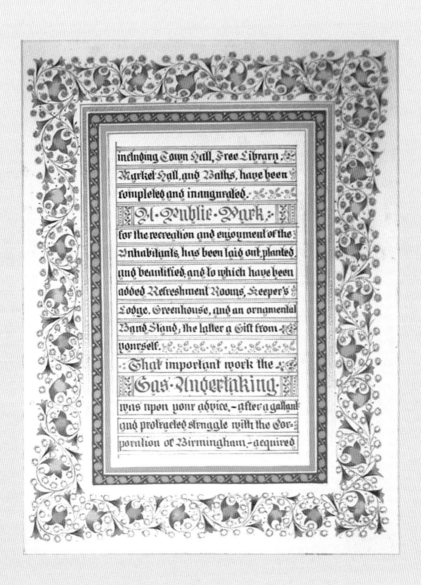

including Town Hall, Free Library,
Market Hall, and Baths, have been
completed and inaugurated.

A · Public · Park ·

for the recreation and enjoyment of the
Inhabitants, has been laid out, planted,
and beautified, and to which have been
added Refreshment Rooms, Keeper's
Lodge, Greenhouse, and an ornamental
Band Stand, the latter a Gift from
yourself.

That important work the

Gas · Undertaking ·

was upon your advice, — after a gallant
and protracted struggle with the Corporation of Birmingham, — acquired

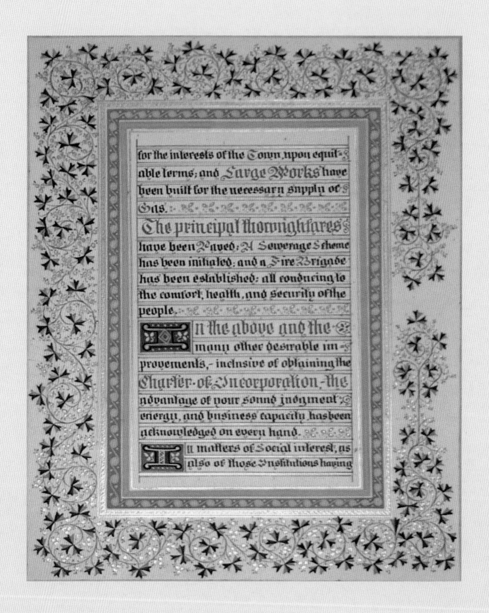

for the interests of the Town, upon equitable terms; and Large Works have been built for the necessary supply of Gas.

The principal thoroughfares have been Paved; A Sewerage Scheme has been initiated; and a Fire Brigade has been established: all conducing to the comfort, health, and security of the people.

In the above and the many other desirable improvements,—inclusive of obtaining the Charter of Incorporation—the advantage of your sound judgment, energy, and business capacity has been acknowledged on every hand.

In matters of Social interest, as also of those Institutions having

XIV

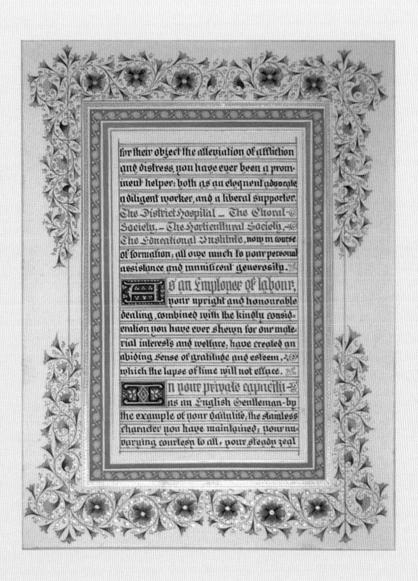

for their object the alleviation of affliction and distress, you have ever been a prominent helper; both as an eloquent advocate a diligent worker, and a liberal supporter. The District Hospital — The Choral Society, — The Horticultural Society, — The Educational Institute, now in course of formation, all owe much to your personal assistance and munificent generosity.

As an Employer of labour, your upright and honourable dealing, combined with the kindly consideration you have ever shewn for our material interests and welfare, have created an abiding sense of gratitude and esteem, which the lapse of time will not efface.

In your private capacity as an English Gentleman—by the example of your habitlife, the stainless character you have maintained, your unvarying courtesy to all, your steady zeal

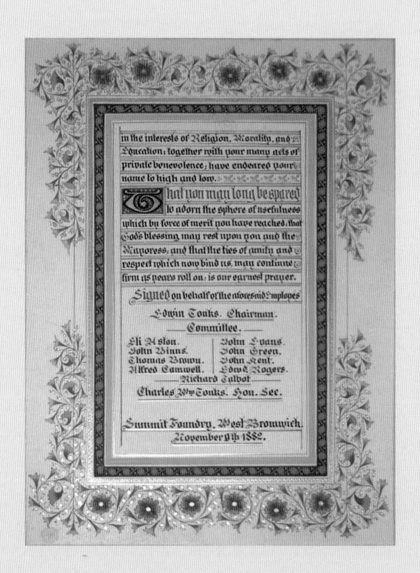

in the interests of Religion, Morality, and Education; together with your many acts of private benevolence; have endeared your name to high and low.

That you may long be spared to adorn the sphere of usefulness which by force of merit you have reached, that God's blessing may rest upon you and the Mayoress, and that the ties of amity and respect which now bind us, may continue firm as years roll on, is our earnest prayer.

Signed on behalf of the aforesaid Employes

Edwin Tonks, Chairman.
——— Committee. ———

Eli Aston.	John Evans.
John Binns.	John Green.
Thomas Brown.	John Kent.
Alfred Camwell.	Edwd Rogers.

Richard Talbot

Charles Wm Tonks, Hon. Sec.

Summit Foundry, West Bromwich.
November 9th 1882.

XVI

CHAPTER FIVE

First And Five Times Mayor

THE ONLY PERSON FOR THE JOB

THE CHARTER OF INCORPORATION 1882

On Monday, the 17th July 1882, the West Bromwich Improvement Commissioners held a "Special Meeting" at their offices in the Town Hall, West Bromwich, "to make certain alterations to the draft charter" which was amended and forwarded to the Privy Council. The Commissioner's Minutes record:

"That the Petition of the inhabitant householders of West Bromwich to the Queen in Council to grant a Charter of Incorporation for the parish of West Bromwich, creating it a Municipal Borough under the Municipal Corporation (New Charter) Act of 1877.

"Witness ourself at our Palace at Westminster the thirteenth day of September in the forty seventh year of our reign. By Her Majesty's Command."

Signed by Cardew with the Grand Seal.

The Returning Officer reported that all the Councillors elected on the 1st. November instant have duly qualified. Moved by Mr. Councillor Underhill seconded by Mr. Councillor Cooksey supported by Mr. Councillor Jackson and Mr. Councillor Blades and resolved unanimously;

"That Mr. Councillor Reuben Farley be elected Mayor of this Borough. Mr. Councillor Farley duly qualified as Mayor of the Borough. The Mayor returned thanks for the honour conferred upon him. The Mayor signified in writing to the Council the appointment by him of Mr. Councillor Underhill as Deputy Mayor."

The Charter of Incorporation was granted to the town on 13 September, 1882, establishing it as a Municipal Borough with its own Mayor, six Aldermen, eighteen Councillors and a Coat of Arms, inscribed with its motto *Labor Omnia Vincit.*

Ref: Committee Minute Book, February 1882 – July 1884.

FIRST MAYOR OF WEST BROMWICH

The Mayoral Chain

The Earl of Dartmouth presented the first Mayoral chain in 1882. Made from 18-carat gold, it bore the armorial bearings of the Earl, Lord of the Manor of West

Bromwich. The oval medallion at the front displayed the arms of the borough and the motto "Labor omnia vincit" enamelled in gold.

THE SILVER MACE

Reuben Farley himself presented the Silver Mace to the borough as minuted on November 17th, 1882.

> Returning Officer in the Elections held under the Charter
> J. Arthur Kenrick Esq returned thanks
> The Mayor offered to present a Silver mace to the
> Borough which offer was received with acclamation.
> The Mayor invited the members of the Council to
> meet him in the Council Chamber on Sunday next
> the 12th instant at 10:45 a.m. and walk with him
> in procession to Christ Church
>
> Reuben Farley
> Mayor
>
> November 17th 1882

The Mace was the symbol of the Mayor's authority and would be carried on formal occasions by the Mayor's Sergeant at Arms or the Mace Bearer who preceded the Mayor. The lower part of the mace was decorated at intervals with appropriate emblems, the words "The Mace of the Borough of West Bromwich" and the crest of the donor.

In Reuben's case the crest used appeared to be the religious symbol of the Lamb and the Cross.

TOLLIT – PECCATA – MUNDI
"He who takes away the sins of the world"

This crest also appeared on many items relating to Reuben. It was used as his badge on the Chain of Office; on the Silver

Cradle presented to him and his wife on the birth of their daughter in 1894; on the Farley family headstone at Christ Church; and was included in the Illuminated address presented to him by his employees at the Summit Foundry.

The Mayoral Robe And Hat

The Borough Surveyor, John T. Eayrs, on behalf of the Officers of the Corporation, presented the Mayor and the Corporation with the Mayoral Robe and Hat as a mark of appreciation of the valuable services rendered by Reuben to the town as Chairman of the Improvement Commissioners.

A SILVER CRADLE PRESENTED TO
THE MAYOR AND MAYORESS OF WEST BROMWICH
Extract from The Weekly News, Saturday, October 27, 1894

On Tuesday evening the Mayor and Mayoress of West Bromwich (Alderman and Mrs. Farley) were presented with a massive silver cradle in commemoration of the birth of a daughter during their year of office. The interesting ceremony took place in the Council Chamber at the Town Hall. Prior to the presentation being made the large company present had tea, after which the Ex-Mayor (Councillor C. Akrill) occupied the chair.

Amongst those present, in addition to the Mayor and Mayoress, were Alderman T. Underhill, J.H. Blades, T. Rollason, and E.W.W. Heelis, Councillor Pitt; Chief- Superintendent Whitehurst, the Town Clerk (Mr. A. Caddick), Mr. T. Hudson (Mayor's Secretary), &c.

Councillor Akrill said they were met together that afternoon to perform a most pleasant and interesting ceremony. As they all knew on 21st August last a little stranger made her appearance in the home of their mayor and mayoress, and many words of congratulation were sent to them on that occasion. He was quite sure that no congratulations were more sincere than those which went from that Council, and he could venture to say more acceptable.

It was customary that a silver cradle should be presented, and the Town Council was not backward in taking that opportunity of presenting the mayor and mayoress with a silver cradle. A meeting was immediately called, and a discussion ensued as to what would be the best method of the presentation. At first it was suggested that the subscriptions should be confined to the members of the Council meeting, and then again it was suggested that it should be confined to the Borough Bench as well as the Council, and thirdly, that the matter should be thrown open to the town. However, after all these suggestions had been made, the Council were unanimous in confining it to the members of the Council only. Objections had been made to the effect that it should be thrown open to the town, but if the townspeople were desirous of celebrating the event, there would be abundant opportunities in the near future.

He did not know that it was necessary for him, in making the presentation, to speak of their esteemed Mayor. They all knew him, and moreover knew what he had done for the town of West Bromwich. They should always be indebted to him as long as West Bromwich was in existence for the work he had done in it. He had been the means of making the town a success, and his name stood, and always would stand, good in the town.

He (Mr. Akrill) was one of those who had to present the Mayor with a requisition signed by every member of the Council, to accept office for the coming year. He knew that Alderman Farley said last year that he should not take office again, as his attention was called to his home, wife and family, and that he was not so young as he once was. He assured them, as one of the deputation, there was only one thing that would reach the Mayor's heart. He had been instrumental with Alderman Heelis, with the Agricultural Society to hold their annual show in West Bromwich, and on such an important event it would require them to have a great deal of confidence, and the Council had not sufficient confidence in anyone but Alderman Farley, as they knew the duty would be carried out properly. This reason weighed very much with him and he again decided to accept the office. Therefore they were all very much indebted to him.

Without making any further remarks he at once proceeded to make the presentation. In doing so he remarked that he had the great pleasure in asking his acceptance of that silver cradle. He hoped it would be regarded as an heirloom, and handed down to his family. He sincerely hoped his life would be prolonged to continue his successful career, and that would be an ample reward to them.

On the cradle was the following inscription: *"Presented to Alderman and Mrs. Farley (Mayor and Mayoress of West Bromwich) by the members and officers of the Town Council, as a token of sincere friendship and esteem on the occasion of the birth of a daughter during their year of office. August 21st, 1894."*

It also bore the Mayor's private crest and the Borough Coat of Arms.

Alderman Farley, upon rising to return thanks, was loudly cheered, and said on behalf of his wife as well as himself he had to return sincere thanks for the presentation. He was proud to be the father of four children. The gift would remind him of the kindness the members of the Council and the Corporation Officials had always shewn him. The cradle would serve as a further link to bind his wife and himself to the borough of West Bromwich. He assured them that that cradle would be regarded as an heirloom, and be handed down to his family.

Alderman Underhill and Blades also spoke of the excellent work which Alderman Farley had done for the town. The company then inspected the cradle, after which the proceedings terminated. The steps leading to the Council Chamber had been prettily decorated for the occasion with chrysanthemums and other kinds of flowers; the corridors and Council Chamber being also decorated.

The cost of the cradle was £100, and the work was executed by Messrs. Elkington and Co., of Birmingham.

CONTEMPORARY REPORTS

BAZAAR AT WEST BROMWICH BAPTIST CHURCH
Extract from The Weekly News, Saturday, September 29, 1894

On Tuesday afternoon a two day bazaar was opened in the Town Hall for the purpose of raising money to liquidate a debt amounting to £1300 at present existing upon the Baptist Church, Lower High Street, West Bromwich. The opening ceremony was performed by the Mayor (Alderman Reuben Farley), and there were also present the Rev. A.W. Oakley (pastor), Councillor, C. Akrill; Messrs.J. Lawley, M. Dunn, &c.

The Rev. A.W. Oakley (Pastor) briefly explained the object of the bazaar, and said it was the expense attending the erection of their new church which brought them there that day. They all knew the old church was very dilapidated, and it rendered it absolutely necessary that they should rebuild it. They had with them that day one who had filled the position of Chief Magistrate and chief citizen of the town three times.

The Mayor's name was a household word in West Bromwich. He then called upon the Mayor to declare the bazaar open.

The Mayor, who met with a cordial reception, remarked that he sincerely hoped that the unfavourable weather would not interfere with the financial result of the bazaar. The object of the bazaar, as explained by Mr. Oakley, was to lessen the debt which had been raised upon their church.

The Mayor of West Bromwich had a good many functions of various characters to perform during his term of office, but he thought that that was one of the most pleasant. Before he sat down he should have to offer an apology for his wife, who was away from home and was also not in the best of health. He did that very sincerely as she would have been pleased to attend. In conclusion he wished them, from the bottom of his heart, the greatest success, and hoped they would realise to the full the amount they had set out to work for. Owing to the absence of his wife he asked to be allowed to make a donation to the funds.

The Rev. C. Cuthbertson proposed a vote of thanks to the Mayor for his presence that afternoon, and in doing so said that apology for his wife touched them all. Mr. Dunn expressed his delight in seconding the vote of thanks, and said when the Mayor was with them the work was sure to be done.

Councillor Garratt said it gave him very great pleasure to support it. He seldom met with such a prompt willingness than the Mayor (had) shown when he asked him to open their bazaar that afternoon. He had scarcely said half-a-dozen-words when the reply came, "Yes." He desired to take that opportunity of personally thanking the Mayor for his kindness in opening the bazaar. They also had to thank him for a donation of £5.

The resolution was then submitted and passed unanimously. The Mayor returned thanks and said he thought he was indebted to West Bromwich instead of West Bromwich being indebted to him. He sincerely hoped they would realise

£400. The sales were then proceeded with, all the stalls being heavily laden with useful and ornamental articles, and they were also handsomely decorated.

The bazaar was continued on Wednesday and was opened by Councillor George Garratt. During both days a host of entertainments and amusements were provided. All of these were patronised most extensively by the numerous visitors, and through their means a substantial amount was added to the previous day's takings. The ladies and gentlemen who worked so hard for the success of the bazaar are to be congratulated upon the prosperous outcome of their endeavours, and we sincerely hope that the debt which is hampering the Baptist Church will be speedily removed altogether.

CHURCH BAZAAR IN WEST BROMWICH TOWN HALL
Extract from The Weekly News, Saturday, October 13, 1894

On Wednesday afternoon an attractive three days' bazaar, or what was described as a "Normandy Fair," was opened in the Town Hall, West Bromwich, the object in view being to raise about £500 to liquidate the debt incurred by the erection of a vicarage at St. Andrews Church, Old Meeting Street.

The opening ceremony was performed by the Mayor (Alderman R. Farley), in the presence of a large attendance. Amongst those present were Mrs. Farley, the Revs. H. Jesson, F. Watkiss Jones, J.B. Crump (vicar of St. Andrews), Alderman T. Underhill, Councillor Chesshire &c.

The Rev. J.B. Crump (vicar) explained the object of the bazaar, but before doing so said that the Mayor had very kindly attended to preside on that occasion, and they were all very grateful to him. He took that opportunity to thank the architects for the trouble and time they had taken in the erection of the vicarage, and also the contractor, who had very carefully carried out the architects' ideas.

Alderman Farley, in declaring the bazaar open, said he was very sorry the weather was so unfavourable, but sincerely hoped it would not keep visitors away from the bazaar, and that it would not suffer by it. He was pleased that they had got such a good vicarage for the parish of St. Andrew's, and he sincerely hoped that the Vicar and his wife and family might spend many happy years in it. He did not know, after the observations which had fallen from the Vicar, that it was necessary for him to detain them. They knew that the vicarage had been erected owing to the generosity of the Revs. R. and H. Jesson, who kindly gave them the land which formed the site. He had said on many previous occasions that the Mayor, during his term of office, had a good many duties to perform, and that was one of the most pleasant, and he thought that remark might apply that day. He sincerely hoped that their anticipations would be fully realised. He had great pleasure in declaring the bazaar open.

Alderman Underhill said a very pleasing duty involved upon him in proposing a vote of thanks to the Mayor for his attendance that day, and for opening the bazaar The Mayor had always been ready to go anywhere, and to help them as much as possible. They all felt very grateful to the Mayor for the kind remarks which he had made. Mr. Horton seconded the vote of thanks, and remarked that the Mayor had always taken a great interest in bazaars and church work. The Rev. J.B. Crump here said he should like personally to thank Alderman Farley, and added that there had not been one occasion when the Mayor had refused to help him. The motion was carried unanimously.

The Mayor said it was rather difficult to respond to a vote of thanks, especially when it had been proposed by Dr. Underhill. He did not know how to express his sincere thanks to them for the hearty manner in which they had carried it. He hoped the results would be to the brightest of their expectations. The sales were then proceeded with, all the stalls which were prettily decorated, being well stocked with useful and fancy articles, and were presided over by the ladies who were attired in Norman costume. During the afternoon and evening Mr. J. Henley's orchestral band rendered selections of music in a capital style.

MAYORAL CONVERSAZIONE AT WEST BROMWICH
Extract from The Weekly News, Saturday, October 27, 1894

Although it was understood when Alderman Farley accepted the Mayoralty of West Bromwich for the fourth time, to relieve the Town Council of a difficulty, that the year would be a quiet one, so as to make it easy for his successors, the Mayor's Conversazione has become an event of such importance in the social life of the borough that general regret would have been expressed had it been allowed to drop out of the festivities of the year. When it became known that Alderman Farley had decided to issue invitations for a conversazione, it was believed that it would be carried out with all his well-known liberality; and those who witnessed the magnificent gathering in the Town Hall on Thursday evening and participated in the evenings enjoyment, must pronounce it a brilliant success, notwithstanding the many excellent gatherings of a similar character which have preceded it in recent years.

About 1000 invitations were accepted, but owing no doubt to the very inclement weather, only about 650 were present. These included the popular borough member Mr. Ernest Spencer, and his wife, the Mayors of Dudley and Wednesbury, the Chairmen of the neighbouring Local Boards, and all the chief citizens of West Bromwich.

The Decorations

Most elaborate preparations had been made to make the entertainment worthy of the occasion. Every available room in the public buildings was utilized, and all were excellently fitted and furnished. The covered awning at the entrance to the Town Hall – plants and foliage hiding the steps on either side – was exactly on the same scale as last year. Just inside the entrance doors was a bank of ferns and flowers, which were most artistically arranged. The various offices of the officials of the Corporation on the right and left side of the corridor were utilised as cloak rooms.

The decorators paid special attention to the Town Hall, or what we may term the ball-room, the floor being covered with parqueterie, and made to represent inlaid wood, in place of the usual diaper, whilst all round and underneath the galleries were luxurious crush rooms and lounges, which were tastefully furnished with settees, couches, easy chairs, large mirrors, gossip tables, etc. This alone gave a look of ease to the place, whilst the floor outside the parqueterie was covered with Oriental rugs, which gave it a warm and comfortable appearance. The walls were picturesquely draped with art muslins and large mirrors, and the doorways and other parts of the hall were hung with tapestry curtains.

The orchestra itself presented a lovely appearance, Mr. Browne, the park keeper, excelling himself with the beauty of the arrangement of the flowers and plants. In the background were fan-like tropical palms, which on account of their singular gracefulness, are everywhere a principal piece of decorative material. Flowers and plants of various kinds were also prettily arranged in the crush rooms.

Messrs. Best and Lloyd, of the Cambary Works, introduced something new to the attractions of the company, there being arranged at the rear of the Town Hall a large pendant which threw a splendid cast upon the dresses near to it, the light could also be subdued to the sight of the people in the crush rooms near to it. The hall as a whole presented a very lovely and charming appearance.

As in former years the Town Hall was connected with the Institute buildings by means of a covered sub-way across Lodge Road. All through this subway and the Institute corridor right to the Lecture Theatre, was one beautiful avenue of trees, flowers, and various kinds of plants. In the Institute buildings two rooms on the ground floor were used as card and smoke rooms for the gentlemen, while the large room reading room was utilised for a refreshment room. Gas pendants and other kinds of lighting apparatus were in abundance, and tended to make the decorations more handsome. The steps up to the Council Chamber were also magnificently decorated. The decorations and furnishings were carried out by Messrs. Norton and Company, Birmingham, under the personal supervision of the manager, Mr. H. Browne, superintendent of Dartmouth Park.

The Reception

Although the decorations of the building can be made to have a striking effect, nothing can equal the brilliance of a well-dressed and well-arranged assemblage of people. The Mayor who wore his chain of office, and the Mayoress received the guests as they arrived, in front of the orchestra, from 7-30 to 8-30, and received a hearty welcome. The variety of colour of the ladies' dresses as they collected round the reception dais, and the remarkable manner in which they seemed to harmonise with the decorative arrangements, made the spectacle an imposing one, and the centre of the hall was one of brilliance, variety, and beauty. The refined enjoyment and merriment reigned supreme amongst the assemblage.

During the reception the Borough Organist (Mr. Wm. Hartland) gave one of his best recitals on the organ; at 8-30 dancing commenced to the strains of Messrs.

Rogers and Priestley's band, and the magnificence of the scene then reached its heighth. The Mayor and Mayoress seemed particularly happy, and entered into the enjoyment of the evening in a hearty manner. Mr. Reynolds, of Birmingham, officiated as M.C., and a number of gentlemen acted as stewards.

The Entertainments

Those not caring for dancing were amply provided for in the shape of dramatic and other entertainments in the Lecture Hall of the Institute Buildings, and in the Council Chamber. At 8-30, in the Lecture Hall, an amateur dramatic performance took place. Later in the evening a dramatic performance took place in the same buildings. Between these two pieces there was dramatic, humorous, and musical recitals.

The refreshments were supplied by Messrs. Lissiter and Miller, of Birmingham, and these were all served in first-class style, there being an abundant supply. The mayor and mayoress were busy among their guests the whole evening, and the silver cradle presented to them on Tuesday being on view, was the object of much admiration. Shortly after twelve o'clock the guests departed, having had a thorough and enjoyable evening's entertainment.

BANQUET TO THE MAYOR OF WEST BROMWICH

Extract from The Weekly News, Saturday, November 10, 1894

Last night a banquet was given in the Town Hall, West Bromwich, to Alderman Farley, the Mayor of the Borough. Councillor Akrill, (ex-Mayor) presided, and on his right was the guest of the evening, and on his left Mr. Ernest Spencer, M.P.

Among the large company present in addition were the Mayor of Dudley (Alderman G.H. Claughton), Mr. Fred Ryland, County Councillor J.B. Lees, Mr. W.H. Lloyd, (ex-Mayor of Wednesbury), Mr. T. Spencer, Mr. F.T. Jefferson, Aldermen Underhill, Councillor G. Salter, the Town Clerk Mr. A. Caddick.

The Chairman proposed, "The Queen." He remarked that as time rolled on their hearts were drawn more and more in attachment to their noble Queen, who was not only the greatest monarch, but the greatest sovereign that had sat upon the throne. Miss Mary Jones than sang the National Anthem. Then the Chairman proposed "The Prince and Princess of Wales, and other members of the Royal Family."

Mr. H.A. Pearson proposed "The Houses of Parliament," and in doing so said they had met to pay homage to one of West Bromwich's most noble sons, who had done more than any other man to promote the welfare of his native town, and they rejoiced to see him sitting there in the full possession of health and strength and manly vigour and they trusted he would be long spared to sit among them.

The Borough Member was well received upon rising to respond. He thanked them heartily for the way the toast had been received, and he went on to say how pleased he was to see Mr. Alderman Farley once again occupying the Chair of Chief Magistrate of the Borough. It was no new position but it was one he had filled before with singular dignity and ability. He ventured to say without contradiction that on each occasion of his Mayoralty he had added greatly to his own reputation as a municipal administrator, and had increased respect for the town of West Bromwich. He complimented the Mayor on the conclusion of a most successful year.

The Chairman next submitted the toast of the evening, "Our Guest." He remarked that it was impossible to say anything new in proposing that toast, but he would like to mention one thing which they all admired Alderman Farley for. It was the act of taking office for the fifth time, which took a great deal of time, but he made the sacrifice and placed himself at the disposal of the town for another year. He had done this so that he might do all he could possibly do in the ensuing year for the purpose of raising the town in which he lived. There were some towns content to remain the same as 25 years ago, but the government of West Bromwich had been placed in the hands of men who had the spirit of progress, men who had proved themselves successful in life, and the manner in which they discharged their duties and responsibilities infused into others the spirit of progress, and raised a high standard.

In West Bromwich they had their parks, recreation grounds, their technical schools, their swimming baths, their streets well paved, and the sanitation welfare of the town was good; so that he claimed in West Bromwich as the pioneer and leader in those things their worthy Mayor.

He knew that the toast would be received with heartiness, and in conclusion he expressed the hope that Alderman Farley would be long spared with health and happiness, and also that of his young family.

The Mayor on rising to reply was enthusiastically received. He said he felt overwhelmed by the flattering manner in which his health had been proposed, and the hearty manner in which it had been received, and he wished he was more worthy of the reception which West Bromwich people had always shown towards him. It was not his desire to continue in office another year, and it was out of deference to the opinions and wishes of his colleagues that he had consented to go on to do his duty. He did not propose to comment on the work of the Sanitary and Highway Committee, as it had been referred to by Mr. Akrill, except to mention that they had spent £40,000 in paving the streets, which they proposed to do from one end to the other.

One thing which had not been mentioned, which he wished to refer to, was that another lodge had been built to the park. They would recollect when the ground was given to them by Mr. Nicholls, the work could not be proceeded with until now, in consequence of mining subsidence's, and he felt that everyone who visited the park would appreciate the improvement which had been made.

The transfer of the Technical Buildings as a free gift to the town was a matter to which they were greatly indebted to Mr. Fred Ryland. That building cost about £12,000, defrayed by voluntary contributions, and while other towns who had adopted the Technical Instruction Act had been compelled to erect buildings, they had that magnificent pile of buildings to handed over to them without any cost to the ratepayers, and today West Bromwich was richer by that £12,000 than it otherwise would have been but for the enterprise and liberality of West Bromwich men, and those interested in the progress and welfare of the town.

He did not wish to say anything of a controversial character about technical instruction, but he did say, and he thought everyone would agree with him, that the youth of their borough ought to be as well equipped in scientific knowledge as they are in any other town in the kingdom. When they considered the keen competition of other countries, and the growing population of the country, how were they to hold their own unless they were properly equipped, so that it was of the utmost importance that their youths should be properly educated in scientific, artistic, and technical knowledge.

He would also like to refer to the acquisition to the town of the old Oak House. They knew that the house was one of the most remarkable of the kind in the kingdom, and a fine specimen of the architecture of the 16th century. Antiquarians and archaeologists came from far and wide to inspect the building, and by and by it would be within the reach of the burgesses of West Bromwich to go over. He agreed with the desire that it should for a limited time be set apart as a gallery for works of art that might be bequeathed to the town until the time should arrive when West Bromwich was in possession of a Museum and Art Gallery of its own. He hoped soon to see that time, and to have the opportunity of lending a helping hand to it.

There was another generous gift which was his privilege to bring before the Council, and that was from a family which was highly respected in West Bromwich, he referred to a the gift of a park in Spon Lane by Messrs. Kenrick. There was no ward in West Bromwich where there were more of the artisan classes than in that ward. West Bromwich was greatly becoming being built upon, and it was very important that they should secure these open spaces, as he believed they exercised a great deal for good upon the rising generation, and it was impossible to go through the beautiful and well-ordered grounds without them having an influence upon their life and conduct. In conclusion he wished to return them his hearty and grateful thanks for the distinguished honour which they had conferred upon him, an honour and distinction which he should never forget.

Mr. J.B. Lees submitted "The Mayor and Corporation." It was necessary he said for him to refer to those excellent qualities which distinguished the past and present career of their worthy Mayor. The best testimony of his prudence, sagaciousness, foresight, and administrative ability was found in the fact that during the comparatively short history of the Council that he had been elected five times to the dignity of Mayor. He had discharged his duties in the same spirit in which he had always performed every public duty since he entered upon public life. He had not only done what he had pledged himself to do, but he had done a great deal more.

There had been running alongside his official duty a noble and generous impulse. He had not only gained the golden opinions of the inhabitants by his force of character, but there had been the pulsation of a larger heart, beating quicker and quicker as the years have gone by, and an earnest desire to do something to uplift his native town, and to improve the condition of his fellow citizens; to make their lives brighter. He had carried out his work in a most disinterested spirit. He had not sought for any of those honours which had come to many who had done less public service.

There were thousands of women and children in their midst who held him in the highest esteem and affection, and he anticipated a time, although the Mayor might not live to see it, when his two sons if they should be spared, and stood where some of them stood that night, it would be their proudest boast that they had a father who lived an unselfish life, and was enrolled in the affection of the people.

They all wished for the Mayor and Mayoress, during the coming year, an uninterrupted course of health, and that they would have increasing joy in their family life; that their official duties would not be a heavy burden, but rather a pleasure. Councillor Salter responded. The Town Clerk proposed the "Health of the Chairman (Councillor Akrill)", to which the latter gentleman responded.

The orchestra was beautifully decorated with choice plants and flowers by Mr. H. Brown, the park-keeper. Mr. William Hartland played a selection of music during the dinner, which was served in excellent style by Messrs. Lissister and Miller, of Birmingham. Miss Mary Thomas sang charmingly a number of selected songs.

CHAPTER SIX

His Good Works

The discovery of several inscribed keys and trowels in the West Bromwich Civic Collection led to further research into the dates and details of the events inscribed on them. The following extracts from The Weekly News record Alderman Reuben Farley's interest and involvement with the design of these churches, buildings and parks which are still with us today as part of our town's heritage.

Contemporary Reports on Foundation Stones, Parks and Bandstands, 1876 – 1894

BUILDINGS

NEW CHURCH OF ST. JOHN THE EVANGELIST, WEST BROMWICH
LAYING THE CORNER STONE July 31, 1876
Extract from The Weekly News, Saturday, August 5, 1876

The authorities and friends connected with Christ Church have long since felt a desideratum in the means of worship in the Lyng, West Bromwich, and after considerable exertions a site was purchased, and over £2,000 have been raised towards the erection of a suitable and commodious church, commensurate with the wants of a poor but densely-populated neighbourhood, known as The Lyng. Mr. Elliott J. Etwell, architect, West Bromwich, was instructed to prepare plans for the new church, which will when completed cost about £3,000, and accommodate nearly 500 worshippers. Mr. Arthur Sheasby (Leamington) is entrusted with the building of the edifice.

At one o'clock, on Monday afternoon, the ceremony of laying the corner stone took place, the Rev. Bishop Abraham D. D., officiating. Although the weather was very uncertain, a large concourse of people assembled on the spot, and Mr. Reuben Farley, (Chairman of the Commissioners) was presented with a trowel and laid the stone in the usual manner. The trowel, chastely engraved, bore the following inscription: **"Presented to Reuben Farley Esq. by Elliott J. Ettwell, architect of the new church of St. John, West Bromwich, on the occasion of laying the corner stone, July 31, 1876."** When this part of the ceremony was over, Bishop Abraham delivered a short address. Shortly afterwards the clergy and choir, who all wore white surplices, retired from the platform, singing "Onward, Christian soldiers;" and the ceremony then ended.

The clergy and choir repaired to the Dartmouth Hotel for luncheon. The Chairman proposed, "The health and happiness of the Queen." The toast was drunk. The Chairman then proposed, "The health's of the Bishop and Clergy of the Diocese."

Mr. Reuben Farley, proposing the next toast – "Success to the Church of St. John," said that in the district where they were erecting the new church there was a teeming population, and he thought there would be no difference of opinion upon this point – that wherever there is a large population there ought to be a place of worship connected with the good old Church of England. Since 1871, when the Census was last taken West Bromwich had gone on increasing its population at an average rate of 1,000 persons every year. At the present time the population of the place was 54,000, and it was of paramount importance that the church extension should equally progress to meet the requirements of the people.

Through the courtesy of Mr. Ettwell, the architect, he had the opportunity of inspecting the plans which had been prepared, and there was no doubt in his own mind that the church, when completed, would be worthy of the worship of Almighty God. It was impossible for them to pay too much reverence to their churches, and the one which they had so well commenced would, he was sure, prove to be of lasting benefit to thousands of their fellow creatures.

The toast which was cordially honoured, was responded to by the Rev. H.N. Churton after thanking Mr. Farley for the generous aid he had given in support of the work, the speaker announced that he had received a letter from Lord Dartmouth, who regretted his inability to be present and enclosed a subscription of £100 towards the building fund. The Chairman here stated that the offertory at the stone-laying ceremony amounted to £110, including a handsome contribution from Mr. R. Farley.

Dr Underhill proposed, in eulogistic terms, the health of Mr. Farley, and in doing so, said that there were many men who had the means, the talent, and the opportunities of doing good, but didn't do it. Mr. Farley on the contrary, shone conspicuously for the good he had done in the parish, and he could only say since he (the speaker) had been in the town, Mr. Farley had always taken a deep interest, in the religious and educational welfare of the parish.

Mr. Farley, in acknowledging the compliment, said he considered it a high honour to take part in a ceremony of that description. He could only say that whatever might be his own opinion as to his shortcomings, the people of West Bromwich always looked upon his doings in a favourable light. It was his native town, and if he looked the world over he could not find a place like it. The proceedings then terminated.

Note:
St. John The Evangelist Church ceased to be used in 1960 and was demolished in 1963. A new church, dedicated to the Good Shepherd with St. John Parish Church, was opened in 1968.

ST. PHILIP'S MISSION CHURCH
THE NEW CHURCH AT WEST BROMWICH March 1, 1892
Extract from The Weekly News, Saturday, March 5, 1892

On Tuesday the ceremony of laying the foundation stone of the new church in course of erection in the Beeches Road, West Bromwich, was laid by Alderman Farley. The large and growing population of Christ Church Parish, has rendered some church extension absolutely necessary, and the present church is a temporary one which is being erected, until a permanent church can be built in front of it.

The temporary church will then probably be converted into schools or parish rooms. It will accommodate 350 people, and will be built of brick, in Gothic style of architecture. It will consist of a nave 32ft. by 25ft., a chancel with a transept on one side, and a vestry on the other. It will be an opened timbered roof, and although plain in character, will be built in a substantial manner. The Rev. Mordaunt Crofton, as Vicar of Christ Church Parish, will have the new church under his care, and the Rev. W. Solly will be curate-in-charge. A procession was formed of clergy, members of the choir, and others to the site of the stone laying among those present being the Rev. Mordaunt Crofton, W. Solly, F. C. Witty, and W. Noble, Alderman Farley, Alderman Underhill, W.H. Kendrick, etc.

The ordinary stone laying service of the church was gone through, when Alderman Farley declared the stone "well and truly laid." He was presented with a silver trowel for the purpose bearing the following inscription:- *Presented to Alderman R. Farley J.P., on the occasion of laying the foundation stone of St. Philip's Mission Church, West Bromwich, March 1st, 1892."*

The builders are Messrs. Henry Smith and Sons, West Bromwich, and the architects are Messrs. Wood and Kendrick.

ST. PHILIP'S NEW CHURCH AT WEST BROMWICH, JUNE 13, 1898
FOUNDATION STONE LAYING
Extract from The Weekly News, Saturday, June 18, 1898

On Monday afternoon the ceremony of laying the foundation stone of the new church of St. Philip, in Beeches Road, West Bromwich, was performed by Alderman Farley, J.P., in the presence of a large number of local clergy, and church people of the town.

The building will be of a very substantial character, and will depend for its effect on the proportion of its parts, rather than extravagant ornamentation. It is to be carried out in red bricks with buff Terra Cotta dressings. The contract has been let to Mr. John Dallow, of Blackheath, and the architects are Messrs. Wood and Kendrick, of West Bromwich.

The scaffold poles round the church were gaily decorated with flags and banners, and there was a very large attendance of people interested in the church. A temporary platform was erected in the centre, and there was a procession of the clergy and friends from the Mission Church adjoining.

The usual Church of England Service was gone through for stone laying, and at the proper time Mr. W. H. Kendrick presented a silver trowel, suitably inscribed, to Alderman Farley, for the purpose of laying the foundation stone, at the same time expressing the hope that they would erect a superstructure substantial in all its parts, and fitting to the Glory of God.

Alderman Farley then laid the stone, and two bottles containing copies of the local and Birmingham papers were fixed in the cavity provided for their reception.

The Rev. W. Solly read out a list of the committee and those chiefly engaged in getting the church erected. The Bishop of Shrewsbury, addressing the people assembled, congratulated them all on being present that day and witnessing what was for many of them the accomplishment of a long-standing desire. The site of the church was acquired many years ago. Some years passed before they erected that modest building near them which had served so long and so well as a Mission Church, and which was always regarded as a temporary provision. They had all been looking forward to the time when that Mission Church would be replaced by a more dignified one.

He trusted that the church, of which they were only about to erect a portion, would have its chancel and organ chamber also. They were thankful to have, as the layer of the foundation stone, one who had been such a friend to the church as Alderman Farley. They were thankful that the Mayor of that Borough and some members of the Council were present to assist in that important work in West Bromwich.

That great parish of Christ Church, West Bromwich, had many years ago a much larger population than now, but the parish of St. John's was formed, and they hoped shortly another parish would be established, while the building of that church was a step in the direction of further relieving the Christ Church population.

The Rev. Prebendary Hodgson said it gave him very great pleasure as an old vicar and as a neighbour to be present that day, when they were in full sight of the accomplishment of plans which were conceived many years ago. It was in the year 1881 or 1882 when he approached the late Earl of Dartmouth and asked him if he would give a site on that Beeches estate for the purpose of building a church. His Lordship was always ready to help forward church work, and by return of post he received a letter stating that he had instructed his agent to map out as much land as he required as a site for the church.

The Rev. M.M. Connor heartily congratulated them upon the arrival of that day. He had to move a vote of thanks to Alderman Farley for his kindness in laying the foundation stone, and he remarked that Alderman Farley took the greatest interest in every movement which had for its object the good of the town, and the welfare of those therein. He was willing to help not only in his own parish and church, but there was no church or school in that borough that had not at one time or another received some assistance from him.

The Rev. C.W. Carrington seconded the resolution, and said Alderman Farley on all occasions was willing to stand out and do his duty for the town, and for the glory of God. They were glad to know his name would be associated with that church.

The resolution having been carried heartily, Alderman Farley returned thanks, and said he regarded it as a distinct honour to be able to assist in that good work, and he trusted it would do something to promote the glory of God, and the good of his fellow creatures.

The Rev. Solly moved a vote of thanks to the Bishop of Shrewsbury, and also to the Mayor for kindly acceding to his request to be present. The Rev. Prebendary

Hodgson seconded, and said he was glad to have so auspicious an opportunity of congratulating the Mayor on his election as Mayor of the Borough. The resolution was carried, and the Mayor briefly returned thanks, the proceedings concluding by the singing of the Doxology.

THE WEST BROMWICH INSTITUTE
LAYING THE FOUNDATION STONE

Extract from The Weekly News, Saturday, August 9, 1884

Among the several events which may be said to distinctively mark progressive periods in the history of West Bromwich, Monday, August 4, must take a prominent and foremost place. The effect upon the present generation of the establishment of such an institution as the West Bromwich Institute will be great; its influence upon the next and following generations is incalculable.

It is now some three years since the discussion of an Institute for West Bromwich on the lines of the Midland Institute at Birmingham, was first mooted. The large manufacturers and leading inhabitants of the town took this matter up with considerable spirit. An influential and representative committee was formed, and Mr. Fred Ryland, one of the leading spirits of the movement has become its secretary.

It was estimated that something like £12,000 would be required to purchase a site and erect a building. With regard to the site for the Institute, they could not possibly have secured one more advantageously situated than the plot of land in Lodge Road. It is near the centre of the borough within a few yards of the High Street, in immediate proximity to the public buildings of the town, and so happily situated in relation to the Town Hall and other municipal buildings. It is proposed to open up direct covered communication between the two buildings by means of a movable bridge, reached from the first floor of the Institute to the gallery of the Town Hall.

The architects, are Messrs. Wood and Kendrick, the builder, is Mr. T. Rowbotham. It is commended that the erection and completion of the building will occupy about twelve months, and that the opening of the Institute will take place in time for the winter session of 1885-6.

In the Park

The programme of the day's proceedings comprised the assemblage of the Sunday School children and their teachers, with the public bodies of officials, in Dartmouth Park, the marching in procession to the Institute ground, the laying of the stone, the Mayor's luncheon in the Town Hall, and the supplying of the children with tea at their respective schools.

The crowd commenced arriving in the park with commendable punctuality. The gates and pillars at the main entrance into the park had been gaily decorated with flowers and flags by the indefatigable park keeper. There was a strong body of police here and at the Herbert Street entrance. Of the forty-five schools in the borough who were to be represented in the procession when arranged in order to facilitate operations that thirty four should enter the park by the main entrance and the remainder by the Herbert Street gate. The children of the schools also carried a large number of small flags and bannerets ecclesiastical and otherwise. There was a large number of new bannerets carried by children of the various schools inscribed with "Success to the Institute," "Knowledge is power," "Love and accord" prepared for the occasion.

Mr. Fred Ryland arrived at the rendezvous at 11.45, followed almost immediately by the Mayor, who wore his robe and chain of office, and was greeted with a ringing cheer as he drove along the avenue.

At ten minutes to twelve the signal was given by bugle for forming the procession, and Capt. Caddick took up his position near the refreshment room to marshal the various bodies into their respective positions.

The Dartmouth Park Band led the way. The volunteers then formed up and marched along the avenue, Mayor and his Chaplain following. In due succession was the members of the council, four abreast the Mayor of Walsall, members of the Board of Guardians, members of the School Board, the County magistrates, members of the Institute Committee and of the Hospital Board. The schools followed.

With The Procession

The total unbroken length of the procession could not have been less than a mile–and-half. The pavements each side of the road were crowded with spectators, who also filled all the available windows and points of vantage from which a good view could be obtained. Such a spectacle as that presented while the procession was wending its way along the High Street was one the like of which has not been witnessed in West Bromwich by even the oldest inhabitant.

In the schools included in the procession were children above seven years of age in each school, arranged in Wards. In addition about twelve hundred teachers and three or four hundred adults and children bring the grand total considered to be over 10,000. The Friendly Societies represented in the procession were made up of the several Courts and Lodges.

The Stonelaying

Across various masts erected at the High Street and Lodge Road were a couple of mottoes one bearing the inscription "Success to our Institute" and the other containing the borough motto "Labor Omnia Vincit". Messrs Long and Co, Birmingham, were responsible for the decorations as also for the supply of a great number of the flags and bannerets used in the procession.

The twelve hundred children who had been selected to form the choir took up their places previous to the arrival of the procession which commenced filing on to the road about a quarter after twelve. The band started up the National Anthem which the children joined in singing.

This over, Mr. J.H. Chance on behalf of the Institute Committee presented the Mayor with a handsome silver ivory-handled trowel and ebony mallet supplied by Messrs. Elkington of Birmingham. The trowel bore the following inscription *"This trowel is presented to Alderman Reuben Farley J.P. Mayor of West Bromwich by the members of the General Committee on the occasion of laying the foundation stone of the West Bromwich Institute, August 4th 1884".*

The Mayor said he had to return his sincere thanks to the Committee of the West Bromwich Institute for doing him the honour to ask him to lay the foundation stone of that Institute. He had also to thank them for the trowel which had just been handed to him by Mr. John Chance which by and by would be appropriated to a useful purpose.

According to the programme of the proceedings he found that he was allotted ten minutes to address them and he did not know that he could better occupy the time than by making a few observations with regard to the aim and object of the West Bromwich Institute preceding those observations by a very brief glance at the history of education in West Bromwich. Before the passing of the Elementary Education Act in 1870, a good deal had been done for elementary education in West Bromwich.

After the passing of the Act which was generally known as Mr. Forster's Education Act in 1870 there was a deficiency of school accommodation in West Bromwich in round numbers of about 700. In the early part of 1871 a School Board was elected for West Bromwich and had since provided a considerable amount of good education for the town.

About fourteen years ago Science and Art Classes were established in West Bromwich and affiliated with South Kensington. These classes were still in existence and by and by would be handed over to the Institute. Although a great deal had been done for the diffusions of the blessings of education in West Bromwich, it had long been felt that there was a great need of an Institute similar to the Birmingham and Midland Institute.

In conclusion, he said the Institute intended to combine instruction with amusement, to do something to benefit the people socially, intellectually and morally and to unite together in bonds of empathy and good feeling all who came within the sphere of its influence. Last of all, it should be remembered that the Institute was non-political and non-sectarian as a fundamental principle of its constitution.

The children then sang the hymn commencing "Hark, Hark my soul" after which the Mayor proceeded to lay the stone and to make the customary declaration that it was "well and truly laid". In the cavity beneath the stone was placed a bottle containing copies of the West Bromwich Free Press, Birmingham Post, Gazette and Mail, a list of the General Committee and the Institute inscription and view of the building and current coins of the realm. The stone is of granite and bears the following inscription:

"This stone was laid by Alderman R. Farley, J.P.
Mayor of West Bromwich, August 4th 1884.
Wood and Kendrick, architects; T. Rowbotham, builder"

The cheers with which the conclusion of this ceremony was greeted having subsided, the Bishop of Lichfield offered a prayer. The singing of the hymn "All people that on earth do dwell" brought the proceedings to an end. The children were marched to the respective schools where they were supplied with tea. Mr. Wm. Hartland conducted the choir.

The Luncheon

The gentlemen invited by the Mayor to partake of luncheon with him in the Town Hall commenced arriving within a few minutes of the completion of the stone-laying ceremony. A considerable number of ladies responded to the invitation to witness the proceedings from the galleries, this invitation carrying with it the privilege of viewing the stone-laying from a platform arranged outside the hall.

The reception had been very tastefully and effectively decorated. The luncheon was supplied and served by Messrs. Lissiter and Miller, of Birmingham, in a satisfactory manner. Grace after meat having been said by the Mayor's Chaplain.

The Mayor announced that he had received a letter of apology from the Lord-Lieutenant of the County, (Lord Wrottesley) who very much regretted his inability to be present. He had received a similar letter from Lord Dartmouth who expressed regret that no member of his family could be present either at the ceremony or at the luncheon, and requested him (the Mayor) to apologise for his unavoidable absence.

He then proceeded to propose the first toast, "The Queen", remarking that she was very much loved by all classes of her subjects and might be justly regarded as an example to all the constitutional regions of the world. Alderman Underhill proposed the toast to the "Bishop and Clergy and other Minister of Religion". The Rev. C.H. Jobern responded to the toast.

Before proceeding farther with the toast list, the Mayor said he wished to take that opportunity of presenting a gold medal to their energetic Secretary Mr. Fred Ryland. Mr. J. Arthur Kenrick, Mr. George Salter, himself (the Mayor), and one or two other friends thought there should be some recognition of Mr. Ryland's able and energetic work on behalf of the Institute. And it was thought it would be very nice if he were presented with a gold medal for these services.

It was Mr. Ryland who called upon him with regard to that Institute and he had thrown his whole energies into it, and those who came into contact with him knew what an energetic businessman he was. He was the life and soul of the movement and as a testimony of their appreciation of those services he asked Mr. Ryland to accept a gold medal. The Mayor then handed the medal to Mr. Ryland amidst loud and long continued applause.

Mr. Brogden M.P. then submitted the next toast, "Success to the West Bromwich Institute." Mr. J.B. Chance proposed, "Success to the Town and Trade of West Bromwich." Mr. James Slater proposed what he termed a most attractive toast, "To the Ladies".

Mr. William Hartland played a selection of music on the organ, while the guests were assembling, and during the luncheon.

WEST BROMWICH INSTITUTE
TRANSFERENCE OF THE BUILDINGS TO THE TOWN
Extracts from The Weekly News, Saturday, September 8, 1894

On Monday evening a meeting of the members of the Institute was held in the Lecture Theatre to confirm the heads of agreement between the Trustees of the Institute and the Town Council for the transfer of the building to the town. The Mayor (Alderman Farley), president of the Institute, presided.

The Chairman moved a resolution approving of the heads of agreement for the transfer of the Institute to the Town Council, and giving authority for carrying the agreement into effect.

Application was made to the Town Council and without going into details they all knew the result. He believed it would be a great boon to West Bromwich that the schools should be municipal ones and he considered that the gift being made to the town was a very generous one. He need not detain them further, but he ventured to hope that the resolution would receive their unanimous approval, and that the result would be beneficial not only to this generation but also to future generations.

Mr. F. Ryland in seconding the resolution, remarked that in drawing up the memorandum of agreement the representatives of the Institute had had in view the safeguarding of the interests of the members of the Institute. He thought those who had read the agreement would say that as far as it was possible to do so they had taken care of those interests. He thought it would be greatly to the advantage of the town that the schools should be Municipal Schools.

In all the speeches by the members of the Council he noticed one feeling, viz. that the schools should be well conducted, and it had been advocated also that manual instruction should be given. This was quite right, but if it was to be carried out to the extent it would be necessary to build, and he had been unable to satisfy himself that any other scheme could be proposed which would enable the Corporation to build on other people's land. It was necessary, therefore, to hand over these buildings as a free gift to the Town Council, and then the council would be able to very largely increase the use of the School.

The success of a town was very largely due to its manufacturing concerns. Science teaching came in with every single manufacture in the town. All these manufacturing districts depend for their progress on their being able to take up the newest improvements, and these had been developing very much lately from the Science point of view. It was for these reasons that they gave to the town the building, in order that Science work should be developed.

Mr. W.H. Lloyd, alluding to the clause in the agreement which provided for members of the Institute having the use of one part of the building, desired to know whether this meant rent free, and was informed that it did mean absolutely free of rent. Mr. F.T. Jefferson said he did not rise for the purpose of offering objection or even criticising the scheme, but as a subscriber to the Institute and one deeply interested in the magnificent work which had been done there, and which he believed would continue to be done, he should like to call attention to the ninth clause of the agreement.

If they contemplated the possibility or the probability of additional buildings being required these additional buildings would no doubt, be erected on the adjoining land. He should like to suggest whether it was not possible to stipulate that any additional building erected there should be in character with the buildings now erected. Town Councils and similar bodies were seized sometimes with fits of economy, and it was in the bounds of possibility that in one of such fits buildings would be erected which would not only be a disgrace to the town, but would detract from the noble elevation. He merely threw this out as a suggestion with a view of safeguarding the character of the building.

THE BUILDING NEWS, AUG. 1. 1884.

: Institute Buildings : : West Bromwich : : Wood & Kendrick : Architects :

The Mayor said the suggestion was a very good one, but the conditions in the heads of agreement having passed the Town Council and been approved he did not think they could venture to alter them. Moreover, he thought they must have some faith in the Town Council. He quite agreed with Mr. Jefferson that sometimes a fit of economy did seize hold of a Town Council. He did not think, however, that the Council would be likely to so far forget themselves as to erect buildings not in character with those already existing there. Some of the members of the Council, he thought, would be very careful to take that point into their consideration.

The resolution was then submitted and carried, and the meeting concluded.

NEW BUILDINGS OF THE Y.M.C.A.
WEST BROMWICH
LAYING THE FOUNDATION STONES, June 20, 1888
Extract from The Weekly News, Saturday, June 23, 1888

On Wednesday the public ceremony of laying the foundation stones of the new buildings, to be the home of the West Bromwich Branch of the Young Men's Christian Association took place. The day was most unpropitious; rain falling the greater part of the time the ceremony was being performed.

The main entrance to the lecture hall and gymnasium will be from St. Michael Street, but an entrance is also provided from the back, to give access from Paradise Street, as a special provision in case of fire or panic. The lecture hall and gymnasium will be lighted by windows on both sides, glazed with cathedral-tinted glass, and will be warmed by stoves, but provision is made in the basement for a heating apparatus.

The other rooms are warmed by fireplaces, and special means of ventilation are provided throughout. The buildings are Gothic in style, freely heated, the front being finished with best bricks relieved with stone dressings. The internal woodwork will be stained and varnished, and the walls coloured. The contract for the erection of the buildings without furniture is £1,600, and the work is being carried out by Mr. R. Heelis, under the supervision of the architect, Mr. Edward Pincher, both of West Bromwich.

Ceremony of laying the Foundation Stones

Amongst those present at the ceremony were the Mayor, (Councillor Heelis), Aldermans Farley and Underhill, Councillors Akrill, Salter, and Rollason, the Rev. J. Mason, Messrs. J.B. Lees, J. Dangerfield, E.J. Hunt, H. Thorne, J. Couse.

After singing and prayer, Alderman Underhill, who presided, said they would all very much regret to hear that the president of the great National Association, Mr. George Williams, who was so large a contributor towards that building, was unable to be present. They were met to celebrate the laying of the foundation stones of that building, which was to be a habitation and home for the West Bromwich Branch of the Young Men's Christian Association.

The Rev. J. Mason presented the first trowel to Mr. J. Couse, who was to lay the first stone in the absence of Mr. G. Williams. The Rev. gentleman remarked that Mr. Williams, the founder of the Association, had shown his goodwill to the branch by giving one hundred guineas towards the fund. The Rev. W. Kelly, in presenting the second trowel to Mr. J. Dangerfield, said he had the fullest sympathy with the objects of the Association. Mr. H. Thorne presented the next stone to the Mayor, and said, as representing the National Council of the Young

Men's Christian Association, he had pleasure in presenting that trowel in the name of the National Committee.

The Rev. J. Davis presented the next trowel to Alderman Farley, and in doing so said he was a gentleman whose name had been and was associated with all movements in their borough of a philanthropic character. Alderman Farley then declared the next stone to be well and truly laid. The Rev. S. Taylor presented the next trowel to Councillor Rollason, who performed the ceremony of laying the next stone. The Rev. A.N. Oakley presented the next trowel to Councillor Akrill. The Rev. N.J. Willis presented the next trowel to Councillor Salter. Councillor Salter then declared the stone to be well and truly laid; after which, the Rev. J. Davis, on behalf of his colleague (the Rev. J. Pearce) presented the last trowel to Mr. E. J. Hunt, who performed the ceremony of laying the stone.

Meeting In The Town Hall

In the evening a meeting was held in the Town Hall, under the presidency of the Mayor (Councillor Heelis). There were also upon the platform Aldermen Farley and Underhill, Councillors Akrill, Rollason, and Hartland, and the Revs. J. Mason and J. Davies. Letters of apology were received from the Right Hon. Earl Dartmouth, the Right Hon. Earl of Lichfield, and other gentlemen. The Mayor requested that one verse of the National Anthem should open the meeting, as it was the anniversary day on which Her Majesty the Queen ascended the throne. The secretary, Mr. H. Jones read the Annual Report.

Alderman Farley was the next speaker and commenced by saying that when Mr. Charles Couse called upon him two or three weeks ago to tell him about the arrangements for the stone laying, he asked him to say a few words at the meeting, but when he saw the programme he was surprised to see his name put down as a sort of leading off speech. He comforted himself with the reflection that when an army was going out to war they generally sent out a few light skirmishers. Unfortunately, the weather that afternoon had been very unfavourable, but that would not damp the ardour of the young men. It had been his fortune to be at a great many stone layings of one kind or another, but there was a feature in that day's proceedings he never remembered before. There were no less than eight stones to lay, and on a foundation like that they should have a very strong superstructure.

He shared in the general regret at the absence amongst them of one who would have given them all very great pleasure, the venerable founder of that institution. It appeared that only 44 years had elapsed since he had established the first Y.M.C.A. in London. It must have gladdened the heart of the great philanthropist, George Williams, for it had not been given to every man to see the results of their own labours during their lifetime. What was the object of that Association? As he understood it the object was to permanently benefit the young men both intellectually, spiritually, and physically. The surroundings had a great deal to do with young men.

That he understood was the object of the Association, that it would find a home for young men, and have a good effect upon them as far as life and character were concerned. Although money was not to be despised whether inherited or earned by honest industry, it was really nothing compared to this. It might seem a hackneyed expression but he thought Shakespeare was right when he said, "He that steals my purse steals trash, but he who filches from me my good name take away all I have."

He understood their premises were to have accommodation for physical education, and that there was to be a gymnasium. Years ago the physical training of young men was very much neglected, but he hoped in their day it would not go to the opposite extreme. It was of great importance that their young men should have a good physical education, and he was glad it was included in their programme – and in all sincerity of heart and purposes he would say God speed this excellent institution.

A hearty vote of thanks was accorded the various gentlemen who had assisted in that day's proceedings, on the motion of Mr. Dangerfield, seconded by Mr. Couse, the Mayor briefly responding. During the evening a number of hymns were sung, and Mr. William Hartland played a voluntary on the organ during the collection.

PARKS

DARTMOUTH PARK

Thomas Woollaston was a Police Superintendent who played a key role at the opening of Dartmouth Park in 1878. He wrote a personalised account of the formation, opening and subsequent development of the park. He presented his pamphlet "Historical and Retrospective Review of Dartmouth Park and Its Associations" to Reuben Farley in 1889.

"Dartmouth Park, West Bromwich was originally a part of the old Sandwell Hall park and estate. About the year 1876 it was acquired from its owner, the present Earl of Dartmouth, who gave, absolutely that portion now referred to in trust to Commissioners then acting under the West Bromwich Improvement Act, as a place for the recreation and amusement of the inhabitants of the town and neighbourhood, who were to have free access thereto on all reasonable occasions, subject to arrangements to be made and carried out by such Commissioners or a deputation from their body.

I must observe and call special attention to the fact that to one gentleman, who occupies a high and honourable position in the town, and who takes a deep interest in its welfare, Alderman R. Farley, J.P. much commendative honour in connection with this subject is due. To his earnest and indefatigable efforts may be ascribed all that has been obtained and to him a deep debt of gratitude is owing from the community for his services in their behalf. With him originated the idea of obtaining a 'Public Park'. The prospect of purchasing one was remote, even if possible, and would have entailed a heavy debt on the parish, probably for years. Such an idea could not be entertained. After much anxious thought and deliberation, in the belief that a public Park, at or in the vicinity of West Bromwich, would be conducive to the health and recreation of its increasing population, he studiously applied himself to the task of selecting and fixing upon a convenient and eligible site. In furtherance of his object he pictured to himself an idea and indulged in a wish, which at first perhaps, gave little hope of being realised. His eye had rested on, and he was enamoured with, the grounds now called Dartmouth Park, then forming part of the old Manor Park of the Sandwell Estate. To his mind that would be a magnificent place for the purpose. In truth it was a noble site. But how was it to be obtained?"

Alderman Farley ventured to approach Earl Dartmouth humbly entreating that his Lordship concede a portion of his beautiful grounds to be used as a public park. The response was favourable and Woollaston refers to the formal opening of the park on June 3, 1878 as a red letter day in the history of West Bromwich.

The Earl of Dartmouth was present to authenticate and confirm his gift of the Park and its transfer. The day was observed as one of general holiday and rejoicing, a day to be remembered.

"People were astir early. Those from adjoining towns and districts were present in great numbers in so much that the streets and thoroughfares were unduly crowded.
"Barricades had been erected at various points to divert traffic from those streets required for the passage of the procession from the Town Hall to the Park."

Woollaston supervised the police arrangements and passed along the streets on horseback trying to prepare the way for the passage of carriages. Large numbers of school children and various orders of Friendly Societies arrived and with some difficulty were put into processional order.

The line was headed by two Fire Engines fully horsed and equipped with their brigades extending from the Town Hall to the top of Bull Street. The procession including a line of carriages containing the whole body of Commissioners and the Earl of Dartmouth set off from the Town Hall. They entered the park at the Reform Street entrance.

"The ceremony commenced by the vast assemblage singing the Old Hundredth Psalm. That was followed by the reading of various

documents by officials setting forth the conditions of the deed of dedication of the Park, in trust for the use of the public, after which Earl Dartmouth, R. Farley, Esq., J.P. and others addressed those assembled. The National Anthem having been sung, His Lordship and party left. The approach to the Park and streets being still considerably blocked, I had to make passage and rode in front to Summerfield House, the residence of T. Underhill, Esq., J.P., M.D., where I left the party.

I now returned to the police station, stabled my horse, and took the refreshment I much needed; and having disposed of some official matters, returned on foot to the Park. The sight which there presented itself to my view was something unique, perhaps never to be repeated. The vast multitude of persons assembled had greatly increased during the interval of my absence, and now occupied all available space. Their numbers could scarcely be estimated. All were engaged in joyous mirth, particularly the juvenile portion. Some of the last-named may, most probably in after-times, when recounting the experiences of their childhood or their youth, refer with pleasure and with pride to what they observed on the occasion, when so susceptible of enjoyment. All went well with them and their stories may continue to be related by generations to come."

In 1887, during his third year as Mayor, Reuben Farley again approached the Earl of Dartmouth for more land to extend the park "for the construction and formation of a lake for boating, skating and other purposes". His Lordship again agreed and gave the extra piece of land as a gift to the town in honour of "Her Most Gracious Majesty's Jubilee".

Additions were made to the park over the years. A marble drinking fountain presented by Earl Dartmouth. A bandstand gifted by Alderman Reuben Farley J.P., a refreshment room with shelter. After the expansion of the park to include a lake, pleasure boats and skiffs were provided together with the necessary buildings.

An elaborate shelter erected close to the lake was recorded by Woollaston as:

"The last or most recent building raised on the ground requires special notice. A memorial plate on its front shows that it was erected in the year 1888 by Alderman Farley, J.P. to perpetuate the memory of his deceased wife, Elizabeth Farley. It is an elegant structure on a well-selected site."

Note:

Woollaston's pamphlet was recently reproduced by local historian Mark Barrett for the Friends of Dartmouth Park.

"The park has been provided for the enjoyment of all,
it is hoped all will assist in preserving it".

OPENING OF THE GREETS GREEN RECREATION GROUND
AND READING ROOM

Extract from The Weekly News, Saturday, August 6, 1892

The opening of the Greets Green Recreation Ground, the land of which has been presented by Alderman Farley, and which is situate in Whitehall Road, took place on Monday afternoon, and was made the occasion of a considerable demonstration in that locality. Some thousands of school children headed by their flags marched to the ground and were arranged around a temporary platform. Shortly afterwards the Mayor (Councillor Salter J.P.), accompanied by most of the members of the Corporation, and other public men arrived at the grounds and took up positions upon the platform.

Among those present in addition to the Mayor were the Borough Member (Mr. E. Spencer J.P.), Alderman Farley J.P., Underhill J.P., Blades J.P., Rollason, J.P. & Councillor Hollier, who thanked Alderman Farley on behalf of the committee for having presented the Recreation Ground, said when he took into consideration the object and purpose for which they were assembled on that memorable occasion he felt proud to express on their behalf their heartfelt thanksgiving and acknowledgements to Alderman Farley for his kindness in presenting the ground. The Recreation Ground was not merely for the use of the present generation, but was for the use and pleasure of succeeding generations in that district and throughout the borough.

They all had a high appreciation not merely of this act but of many previous acts of Alderman Farley which had testified to his great generosity to his native town. Having alluded to the Incorporation of West Bromwich, to the Institute, the Municipal Buildings the magnificent Central Free Library, and the Public Baths, he remarked that Mr. Farley would be the last to arrogate to himself anything in the shape of exclusiveness in regard to these works, but he had, nevertheless, taken no undistinguished part in their acquisitions.

Mr. Farley had been in the forefront in regard to all those questions, and they must not forget the gas undertaking which had been a great boon to West Bromwich. In concluding he remarked that the work that was being done that day formed another crowning act of Alderman Farley, who had been so generous to the borough, and it was now his pleasure to hand over to Alderman Farley a beautiful duplicate key of the ground. He explained that the key bore the Borough Arms, Mr. Farley's crest and motto and his initials, and finally he expressed the hope that Mr. Farley might live long to witness the appreciation of his generosity.

Alderman Farley, who was enthusiastically received, said the pleasing and agreeable duty now devolved upon him of asking the Mayor's acceptance of the Greets Green Recreation Ground for the use and enjoyment of the inhabitants of the Greets Green Ward and the Borough of West Bromwich for ever. He said it would be within the recollection of many of them in that year of 1887, when it was proposed to make an extension to Dartmouth Park by the munificent gift of Lord Dartmouth, one or two meetings were held in which some dissatisfaction was expressed that so much money should be spent upon the park and so little on Greets Green Ward.

He sympathised very much with the views and sentiments of the people of Greets Green because they were not able to avail themselves to the fullest extent of the advantages of Dartmouth Park. Feeling that very much, and happening to be Mayor at the time, he conceived the idea that it would be a good thing if Greets Green had a Recreation Ground of its own. His first idea was to give a piece of land at the back of Dunkirk Hall, but after looking carefully at the whole matter he came to the conclusion that that land was ill adapted for the purpose, and looking round the ward his eyes rested upon the spot on which they were now assembled. He held some consultation with the Borough Surveyor (Mr. Eayrs), who was of opinion that it would make a very good recreation ground, and he then obtained the address of the owner, Mr. George Jones, of Kent.

He journeyed to Kent and was well received by Mr. Jones. In matters of this kind there was a good deal of negotiations and at one time he was afraid that the purchase would not come off, but it had finally been effected, and he was bound to acknowledge that Mr. Jones had met him most fairly, and that the price paid was a fair and reasonable one.

Someone might ask why as Mayor of the town he had thought it a proper thing to provide a recreation ground for Greets Green instead of Hill Top. That was very easily explained. In the first place Greets Green was a long distance from Dartmouth Park, and in the second place he was born within a very short distance off where they were assembled and lived in the neighbourhood for 40 years, and he should always cherish a feeling of gratitude for the kindness and consideration he had always received from the inhabitants of that ward.

He sincerely hoped that the inhabitants of that ward would avail themselves to the fullest extent of this ground for physical recreation, and that they would go there, both young men and maidens, old men and children in this generation and many generations to come, and derive benefit and advantage from the means of recreation which had been provided. Places such as that would do something, he thought, to make the lives of the people brighter and happier.

He could not conclude without expressing his gratitude to Mr. Hollier and the committee who had presented him with the beautiful key as a memento of that interesting occasion. He should regard it as an heirloom which would be handed on to his son and when he (Alderman Farley) had passed away he hoped that whenever his son looked at it he would be stimulated to do even more than his father had done for West Bromwich. He then declared the ground open.

The Mayor, on behalf of the town, then accepted Mr. Farley's gift. It gave him very much pleasure to accept this gift, he was sure the town would appreciate it, and that it would be well cared for. Finally, he thanked Alderman Farley in the name of the town.

Alderman Blades next thanked Alderman Farley on behalf of the Park Committee. The speaker humorously remarked that there was no place like Greets

Green he was sure, Alderman Farley was born there, and a good many more great men were born there. Years ago his parents used to set Alderman Farley up as an example for him to follow, and he had followed him as closely and conscientiously as he could, he had dogged his footsteps.

Alderman Farley became a member of the Board of Guardians and he followed him there, he followed him also as Chairman of that important authority. Alderman Farley became a Commissioner and he followed him there; he went on the Town Council and became an Alderman and Mayor and he found him running so hard that he could follow him no longer.

Years ago Alderman Farley made one mistake when he left that ward and went up into West Bromwich, but he (Mr. Blades) followed him, and he expected they had both repented. When Alderman Farley made up his mind to return he also would seriously consider it. He hoped the time was far distant when Alderman Farley would no longer be connected with the public life of West Bromwich.

Mr. E. Spencer, M.P. alluding to Alderman Farley's gift, expressed the hope that the excellent example would be followed.

The crowd then joined together in singing the National Anthem, after which the Mayor, the Borough Member, Alderman Farley, and a number of others proceed to the new Reading Room which had been erected within the ground, for the formal opening, a ceremony which was performed by the Mayor.

The Mayor here mentioned the names of Mr. Long, the architect, Mr. Jonathan Bywater, Mr. J. Butler, Mr. Alderman Blades, Mr. Councillor Browne, and Mr. Councillor Baggott, all of whom he said, deserved their thanks for the part they had taken in the work. Mr. Long, being called for, gracefully acknowledged the compliment that had been paid him, and spoke in admiring terms of the public services of Alderman Farley.

Subsequently about 3000 children, and between 400 or 500 old people were provided with a free tea in celebration of the opening of the grounds. It was

announced during the proceedings connected with the opening of the Reading Room that Alderman Farley had given a cheque for £5.5s towards the cost of this treat.

During the afternoon the Gold's Hill Saxhorn Band, under the direction of Mr. Shephard, played selections of music, and the grounds were very largely patronised.

OPENING OF A BAND – STAND, AUGUST 21, 1894 AT GREETS GREEN RECREATION GROUND.
Extract from The Weekly News, Saturday, August 25, 1894

Generous Offer By The Mayor

Tuesday evening last will be long remembered by the many hundreds of men, women and children who availed themselves of the opportunity of being present in the Greets Green Recreation Ground, Whitehall Road, when a new band stand was formally opened by the Mayor (Alderman R. Farley).

The ground was effectively decorated with flags, etc., and also the band and the entrance for the occasion. The proceedings commenced with a procession from the entrance of the ground to the band stand, which was headed by Messrs. W. and T. Avery's Band. Among those who joined in it was the Mayor (Alderman Farley), Alderman W.W. Heelis and J.H. Blades, the Rev. H. Jesson, (vicar of St. Peter's, Whitehall Road), Messrs. Jonathan Bywater (chairman of the Band Stand Committee), A. Long (architect) &c. The gentlemen entered the band stand.

Mr. Jonathan Bywater, in a few explanatory remarks said the Band Stand Committee asked His Worship the Mayor to receive from them, on behalf of the Corporation, that band stand. The same had been erected by voluntary subscriptions ranging from £10 to 1d. The children in Greets Green he was pleased to say, had contributed no less than £12 to the band stand. Since the Mayor had so kindly presented the recreation ground to them they had felt that they would be very remiss in their duty if they did not provide a band stand, and he was pleased to say the whole thing was being handed over free from debt. It was the wish of the committee that the lives of the people in that particular part of the borough might be made brighter and enlivened by hearing the sweet strains of music, which would from time to time, be discoursed from that stand. They felt sure that they would be satisfied in the future for their labour. It gave him very great pleasure in handing over the deeds and vouchers of the money to £105.

The Mayor said, on behalf of himself and the Corporation of West Bromwich, he accepted from the hands of Mr. Jonathan Bywater that beautiful rustic and artistic bandstand, upon the conditions he had named, that the Mayors and Corporation would keep it in good repair.

He quite agreed with the observations which had fallen from Mr. Bywater, and he hoped the sweetest strains of music would make their lives happier and brighter.

Young men and children would come there for enjoyment and recreation, and Mr. Bywater had truly said they had tried to make the recreation ground complete. As an old resident of Greets Green, he wanted to ask them and Mr. Bywater to allow him the privilege to present them next year with a fountain which he hoped would be very useful. It had been a great pleasure to him, as an old resident in West Bromwich, to do what little service he could. He had spent many years of his life in West Bromwich, and he hoped to carry out the desires of his heart. He was very pleased to see the ground laid out so well. In conclusion he wished them, from the bottom of his heart that they should get all possible enjoyment from it.

Mr. Bywater asked them on behalf of that great gathering to congratulate the Mayor on the birth of a daughter, an event which he was pleased to say took place that morning, and by doing so he wanted them to give three hearty cheers. The crowd then indulged in cheering, after which Mr. J. Butler proposed a hearty vote of thanks to the Mayor for his attendance that evening, and for accepting the gift. The resolution was then submitted and was carried unanimously.

The Mayor responded and was loudly cheered. He also tendered his sincere thanks to those present for the unanimous manner in which they had passed the resolution. His heart was too full for him to say much on that occasion, and he hoped every possible joy and happiness would rest among them in that industrial part of the borough. In concluding he asked them to join with him in giving three hearty cheers for the band stand. This tribute was paid, after which he declared the band-stand open. The band then struck up with "Auld Lang Syne," after which the Mayor and the other gentlemen present were photographed from the band-stand by Messrs. E.J. Timmis, Oldbury Road, Greets Green. We are asked to state that the band-stand, which is of a rustic style, is the work of Messrs. Bayliss and Inman, Stephenson Street, Birmingham. The architect is Mr. Alfred Long, High Street, West Bromwich, and without doubt the stand is one of the largest and most artistic in the Midlands.

At the close a collection was made for the purpose of purchasing about 35 chairs for the band-stand, and also some canvas to shield the band in wet and windy weather.

CHAPTER SEVEN

The Oak House

OAK HOUSE

A picturesque timber framed Yeoman's house dating back to the 16th century. Reeves told us in 1836, "This place takes its name from an ancient Oak Tree that stood on the green in front of the house; it was hollow, and was destroyed by fire about thirty-five years since. Formerly a great many of these Oaks grew upon the estate." Early parish baptism records for this area often showed a family's address as 'near the oak'.

The original owners of Oak House are not known but a family closely associated with it are the Turtons who lived there c1634-1768. Also the Whyley family who occupied the house until 1837. A succession of owners followed until Reuben Farley purchased the property from the Piercy family in 1894.

Perhaps intending to live there, Reuben changed his mind and made a gift of the house for use as a museum and art gallery, "for the free use and enjoyment of the inhabitants of West Bromwich for ever". Renovation was required and West Bromwich leading architects Messrs Wood and Kendrick were employed to restore the house. In the report by W.H. Kendrick to the Chairman & Members of the Estates Committee of the West Bromwich Town Council dated 7 September, 1895 he stated:

"In my opinion, to patch up and repair, merely to make habitable, would entail an outlay of £500. On the other hand, to restore – having due regard to permanence of structure and a non-violation of architectural characteristics, would cost about £1,550." He strongly recommended a thorough restoration. "The very nature of the work to be done is such as demands the most tender and patient treatment, and it would therefore be preferable to take the work in sections, spreading it over at least five years, with a small staff of permanent workmen possessing some technical knowledge of restoration."

If the council had doubts about where the money would be raised they need not have worried as Reuben backed up his gift with the necessary finance too which was confirmed in his letter to Alfred Caddick, the Town Clerk on September 11, 1895.

"Dear Sir,
Mr. Kendrick's report on the Oak House, which you sent me, I have read with much interest. This able and elaborate report bears upon it the impress of having been prepared by a loving hand, a reverential mind, a born archaeologist. I agree with Mr. Kendrick that the right course to

pursue is thorough restoration, and not reparation, although the estimated cost is in excess of what I had calculated upon. As the giver of the Oak House, I should not like the rates to be burdened with the cost of restoration. I shall therefore be willing to undertake the restoration and the adaptation of the pleasure grounds, upon the lines laid down by Mr. Kendrick, and under his supervision, upon the following condition:- That the Oak House shall be dedicated and maintained as a Museum and Art Gallery for the free use and enjoyment of the inhabitants of West Bromwich for ever.

Faithfully yours, Reuben Farley"

Reuben also had plans drawn up for a new street (Cambridge Street) to be built in front of the Oak House running from Bromford Lane to Oak Road. The plans by T. Rollason were approved on September 10, 1895 and indicated a small gate entrance to the Oak House property.

Poem: **OAK HOUSE**

Inside Oak House I stand alone
Now middle years, a woman grown.
Walls of wooden panels shine
The clocks now silent, lost in time.
I'm here to lay my past to rest.
The voices call, the stage is set.
My childhood visits come to mind
Of darkened rooms so hard to find.
Creaky chairs and chests so old.
The walls are bare, the feeling cold.
Its history full with tales to tell
Of preacher, wars and knights that fell.
To see Oak House a child once saw.
Come take my hand walk through the door.
Waiting for the sun to shine.
The sundial stands, its hand in line.
The bowling green forbidden land,
Though great for cartwheels and handstands.
Take a stroll through flowery beds,
A pathway laid for you to tread.
Turn round the house is standing there,
Chimneys high and windows bare
The sun goes down the grounds are clear.
The seasons change now winter's here.

Eerie spotlights shine at night.
The house now stands in ghostly light.
The festive tree so bright and tall.
Branches wide will welcome all.
It's Christmas Eve the carols ring
Inviting all to come and sing.
Here my memories fade away
Like dusk invades a closing day.
My childhood visit here in rhyme
Is captured now and locked in time.

By Lynne Pearce

THE TUDOR HOME OF A YEOMAN FAMILY

From an article on "Old West Bromwich" by W.E. Jephcott. April 21, 1944

In Oak House the town possesses a specimen of Tudor architecture so remarkably preserved in its original form that it may justly be regarded as the outstanding link between the past and the present.

In 1836 a Mr. Habershon of London published an illustrated work on half-timbered houses in the country and of the Oak House said: *"This fine specimen of the ancient architecture of England is nearly embosomed in trees of a full growth and with its groups of high-shafted chimneys, the number and variety of its gables and its beautiful central turret – or more properly speaking its central tower – has a most imposing effect. This tower is the finest thing of its kind in the kingdom. It was perhaps originally used for lighting the hall or staircase although it is now but a common loft. The house appears to retain pretty generally its original appearance and character. The style as indicated by the chimneys and the windows but particularly by the enrichments of the tower, I should consider to be the latter part of the reign of Henry the Eighth."*

That is the description of one who visited it more than a century ago. It is difficult today to realise that it was then "nearly embosomed in trees" which were splendid oaks and one of which of exceptional girth and stature, is said to have caused it to receive its original name of "The Oak".

In "Old Staffordshire Houses" published in 1882, W. Niven said*; "This is one of the most interesting timber-built houses in the country. The brick portions towards the gardens bear indications of having been added at a later date. The hall is entered from the porch and the wing to the right of the hall seems to have contained the private rooms on the ground floor. To the left of it was the kitchen etc. the staircase being entered through a doorway opposite the porch. The picturesque lantern, which is the most characteristic feature of the house, was probably erected chiefly for effect and as a prospect room. Panelling and chimney pieces of the 17th century remain in some of the rooms."*

In another description of the Oak House in 1877 it was said that the first house was entirely half-timber. At the time of its erection one sleeping arrangement almost universally prevailed in yeomen's houses. The farmer occupied the bedroom at the head of the stairs and members of the family and servants took the bedrooms on the different sides, males all going to one side and females the other. In many instances the central room was only separated from the way to the side bedrooms by tapestry curtains.

The great alteration in the Oak House consisted of an enlargement of the western living room, the insertion of a new staircase and a hall with an additional reception room. Hackwood suggests that Thomas Turton, the first to be designated "of the Oak" or his brother John, to whom he sold it, carried out these additions for between 1634 and 1635 the house appreciated in value from £350 to £620. The description from which I am quoting said: *"The designer of the latter portions evidently scorned to be a mere copyist; he boldly erected his additional building in the then prevailing style. Thus we get an excellent example of half-timber construction with a typical addition of later brickwork."*

Reference is also made to the oak pins holding together the massive timbers – nails were not in use then – the moulding on the solid framing nothing like the modern stuck-in mouldings; quaint ironwork and admirably executed carved work in bold and low relief.

The old mansion of the Turton's has seen much national and local history made. Roundhead and Cavalier have tramped its oaken floors and partaken of the hospitality of the residents. John Wesley preached beneath its walls. In his "Journal" he records under date 1774 March 19th, *"At noon I preached at Bromwich Heath and the room being far too small stood in Mr. Wiley's court-yard, notwithstanding the keen north-east wind".* The Room, as it was called, was the original Wesleyan preaching house in Paradise Street, and Mr. William Whyley resided at the Oak House. Apparently Wesley went there again for he wrote *"1779 Sunday March 21st. Just at the time of preaching at Bromwich Heath, began such a storm as that which ushered in the year. Yet as no house could contain the people, I was constrained to stand in the courtyard. For a moment I was afraid of the tiles falling on the people but they regarded nothing but the Word. As I concluded we had a furious shower of hail."*

The Oak House is notable as possessing a secret hiding place. It is a good example of a pivoted panel, situated in the panelling in the side of a passage on the first floor and about four feet from the floor. The space between the panelling and the wall at the back is large enough to conceal a man but the panel is much too small to admit him. Apparently it was used as a place of concealment for valuables or possibly for weapons. In the troubled times of the Civil War it was useful to have a secret place in which articles of value could be concealed without the risk of their being found by any unauthorised persons. Frequent use has made the "secret" panel unmistakable but at one time it must have been almost impossible to distinguish it from any of the others covering the whole wall.

H.V. Morton, whose articles and books descriptive of many parts of Britain are known to most people, came to West Bromwich and "discovered" the Oak House. This is what he wrote, *"Facing the new streets like a man in fancy dress in the middle of a busy road stood a beautiful little black and white half-timber house. I have seen hundreds of Tudor houses up and down the country but I cannot remember a neater, prettier or more appealing example than the one West Bromwich so surprisingly owns. It is a perfect example of the house of a gentleman farmer of the time of Elizabeth. It is a little manor house in miniature. It has a remarkable central tower which must I think make it unique among old houses of this kind in England."*

That is a tribute which should make West Bromwich proud of this possession.

OAK HOUSE FORMALLY HANDED OVER TO THE BOROUGH

Extract from The Chronicle of Friday July 29, 1898

After three years of restoration the Oak House was formally handed over to the town on Monday 25, July 1898. Lord Dartmouth attended the ceremony which commenced with a Luncheon at the Town Hall.

The event was attended by prominent and important townsmen of West Bromwich together with the Mayors of Wolverhampton and Wednesbury.

In his thanks to Mr. Farley for his generosity in donating the museum to the town, Mr. M. Tomkinson refered to Oak House as *"a noble institution, framed as it was in coal dust and smoke and it should become the storehouse of imagination and beauty for all time."* He would remember West Bromwich as long as he lived, not only as a populous town wrapped in mist and smoke, but also as the home of those who considered the welfare of those around them.

Councillor Salter commented on the fact that Alderman Farley, in addition to providing Oak House, had also had a bowling green constructed in the adjoining grounds. Then jokingly said, *"Members of the Town Council, if overdone with their arduous work, might go there and recover themselves. They hoped to see Alderman Farley and the Mayor taking part in a game and he himself might take on Councillor Darby."* Regarding the house which dated back hundreds of years, he hoped it would now exist for many years to come and he had one or two ideas for items which could be included in the museum – *"the eye glasses of Alderman Blades, Councillor Chesshire's cap and the stump of a full flavoured cigar."*

The Mayor, Councillor Pitt, looked back over Reuben Farley's public life. *"One pleasing feature in connection with municipal life was that men of ability, character and wealth shared the public work. Their Corporation had been honoured and distinguished by such men as their host of that day. He had given 40 years of his life in the service of his native town and he had employed his capabilities and given of his wealth towards making West Bromwich what it is."*

Alfred Caddick, the Town Clerk, proposed a toast to the Architects in the restoration of the Oak House, Messrs. Wood and Kendrick. In order to keep the house in the town Alderman Farley spent a large sum of money on restoration and

"THE OLD OAK HOUSE" 1899 Lavinia Benbow
Illustrations by: N. Ault and Katherine O. Underhill (curator of Oak House Museum)

After weathering the storms of ages it stands 'neath its weight of years in grand old beauty'.

had exercised very judicious taste in the choice of the architects. The house was a unique specimen of mediaeval architecture and dated back to a period of great interest in English history such as the time of the fighting between the Crown and Parliament.

One of the architects, Mr. W.H. Kendrick confessed to being a native of West Bromwich and that as young boys he and his partner had played about the Oak House. How fitting then that as men they should have the privilege of being associated with the restoration. When Alderman Farley approached them no question of cost was raised, their commission was to restore the house as they thought it should be restored. They looked upon the house in five distinct periods. Firstly as the owner's house with oaks surrounding it. Then it was almost a garrison of soldiers billeted there after retreating before Prince Rupert at the battle of Birmingham in 1643. It was also thought that soldiers were accommodated there before attacking Dudley Castle. Then it became a gentleman's residence belonging to the Turtons before a period of desolation and now it was restored to its full beauty.

A procession followed the Luncheon and headed by the Volunteer Band they began the route from the Town Hall to the Oak House. People lined the streets which were decorated with bunting and banners.

The area in front of Oak house had been laid out as pleasure grounds for children and upon arrival at the entrance gates Alderman Farley presented the Mayor with a key to officially open them. When he declared the grounds open the Mayor said that he hoped West Bromwich would derive enjoyment from their use forever.

In front of the Museum, Alderman Farley addressed Lord Dartmouth asking him to accept a beautiful key which he hoped would have a place among the curios of his Lordship at Patshull. In considering the opening of the Oak House Reuben said he had thought of only one person, the most fitting person, to discharge the duty and that was the Lord of the Manor of West Bromwich and the Lord Lieutenant of Staffordshire. Lord Dartmouth accepted the key with great pleasure, was grateful for the opportunity of being present and he hoped the pleasant associations of the Dartmouth family with West Bromwich would continue. Voicing the feelings of everyone he acknowledged the deep debt of gratitude everyone owed to Alderman Farley for his generosity and deep public spirit. The best return which they could make for such a noble gift was to take full advantage of it and protect it. He would not go into the history of the house but commented, *"no doubt if the walls could write their history during the last 400 years it would be interesting reading".* His Lordship then formally opened the museum door and admitted the company.

After an official photograph was taken of the party at the rear of the house, a vote of thanks to Lord Dartmouth was proposed by the Mayor. Alderman Blades expressed his gratitude and claimed that in West Bromwich they seemed to think they had a claim upon and a right to the services of the Earl. Perhaps that was due to the fact that for a great number of years his ancestors were closely and intimately connected with West Bromwich and had seen it grow from a small insignificant place to a large municipal borough.

They hoped that his visits would be frequent, pleasant and enjoyable and mutually beneficial.

CHAPTER EIGHT

Everybody Acknowledges His Good Works

ILLUMINATED ADDRESS

FOR THE FIRST MAYOR OF WEST BROMWICH

The Victorians never did things by halves and when Reuben Farley became the first Mayor of West Bromwich in November 1882, all his employees at the Summit Foundry clubbed together to commission an illuminated address.

This was no ordinary framed address but a volume of nine beautifully decorated pages with red leather covers which clipped shut. Executed by E. Morton of Birmingham, it was an exquisite piece of work which must have taken quite some time to complete. Apart from the comprehensive text, several pages included pictures of local scenes such as the public buildings, the market hall, Summit Foundry, the entrance to Dartmouth Park, the bandstand in the park, the public baths and the district hospital.

To Alderman Reuben Farley J.P.
Upon the occasion of his Election as
First Mayor of the
Municipal Borough of West Bromwich
November 9, 1882.

Pg 2   **To Alderman Reuben Farley J.P.** We the employ'es at your Summit Foundry West Bromwich, desire to offer to you our hearty

Pg 3   congratulations upon your election as first Mayor of this Borough. The entire unanimity with which your colleagues elected you to the civic chair and the unqualified approval expressed by all classes of the Townspeople at your appointment to that honourable position, is but one of the many tributes to your high personal character and public worth. As a body of employees we deem it no slight honour to be connected, in however humble a capacity, with one who by his rare qualities and consistent life, has

Pg 4   justly gained such high distinction amongst his fellow men.
The honour in which your name is held is not the glare of a brief popularity but is the result of years of labour and love in the interests of your native town. From your earliest manhood you have in a marked degree, been identified with all the principal movements, having for their object the progress and wellbeing of the town and its inhabitants. In all your undertakings, whether as Chairman of the Guardians

Pg 5   as a member of the first School Board, President of the West Bromwich Building Society, Chairman of the late Board of Commissioners, or any other of the responsible offices you have been called upon to fill, you have by your ability, energy and conscientious discharge of duty, acquitted yourself to the entire approbation of your fellow Townsmen of all classes, without distinction of creed or party. During the past eight years that you were chairman of the Board of Commissioners, many important improvements have been accomplished for the lasting benefit of this place, amongst which the following may be enumerated:

The Public Buildings:

Pg 6 including Town Hall, Free Library, Market Hall and Baths, have been completed and inaugurated.

A Public Park for the recreation and enjoyment of the inhabitants, has been laid out, planted and beautified and to which have been added Refreshment Rooms, Keeper's Lodge, Greenhouse and an ornamental Band Stand, the latter a gift from yourself.

That important work the **Gas Undertaking** was upon your advice – after a gallant and protracted struggle with the Corporation of Birmingham – acquired

Pg 7 for the interests of the Town upon equitable terms and **large works** have been built for the necessary supply of gas.

The principal thoroughfares have been paved, a Sewerage Scheme has been initiated and a Fire Brigade has been established; all conducing to the comfort, health and security of the people.

In the above and the many other desirable improvements, inclusive of obtaining the **charter of incorporation** the advantage of your sound judgment, energy and business capacity has been acknowledged on every hand. In matters of Social Interest as also of those Institutions having

Pg 8 for their object the alleviation of affliction and distress, you have ever been a prominent helper both as an eloquent advocate, a diligent worker, and a liberal supporter.

The district hospital – The choral society – the horticultural society – the educational institute, now in course of formation, all owe much to your personal assistance and munificent generosity.

As an employer of labour, your upright and honourable dealing, combined with the kindly consideration you have ever shown for our material interests and welfare, have created an abiding sense of gratitude and esteem which the lapse of time will not efface.

In your private capacity – as an English Gentleman – by the example of your daily life, the stainless character you have maintained, your unvarying courtesy to all, your steady zeal in the interests of Religion, Morality and Education, together with your many acts of private benevolence, have endeared your name to high and low.

Pg 9 **That you may long be spared** to adorn the sphere of usefulness which by force of merit you have reached, that God's blessing may rest upon you and the Mayoress and that the ties of amity and respect which now bind us, may continue firm as years roll on, is our earnest prayer.

Signed on behalf of the aforesaid employees

Edwin Tonks, Chairman

— -COMMITTEE- —

Eli Aston	John Evans
John Binns	John Green
Thomas Brown	John Kent
Alfred Camwell	Edwd Rogers

Richard Talbot

— — — — — — — — — — — — — — — — —

Charles Wm.Tonks hon.sec.
Summit Foundry, West Bromwich
November 9th, 1882

RECOGNITION OF HIS PUBLIC WORK

In June 1885 Reuben's colleagues of the Town Council recognised to some extent his public work by the presentation of a life size portrait in oils by Mr. Munns for the Council Chamber whilst a replica of it was presented to Mrs. Farley (Mr. Farley's second wife).

Reuben's subsequent generous gift of the Oak House to the town and his continued great public services led to another movement to recognise in a more enduring form of what he had done for West Bromwich. There were various suggestions as to the form this recognition should take but a proposal that he should be made the first Freeman of the Borough was at once taken up with great enthusiasm. On April 20, 1896 the interesting ceremony of conferring this signal mark of honour upon our distinguished townsman took place at the Town Hall. In the presence of a large and very influential gathering the scroll was presented to him in a casket made out of one of the old beams from Oak House and designed by one of the students of the School of Art.

It was soon found that the general public were as desirous as Mr. Farley's colleagues of recognising the services he had given to the town. The West Bromwich Mayor, councillor George Salter led the movement. He held a meeting with leading figures where various suggestions were discussed, from a marble statue to a clock tower. The clock tower was decided upon by a vote of 24 in favour, 13 against. Then came the question of where to erect it? Possible sites were Dartmouth Square (top of Spon Lane), Mayers Green (near the entrance to Dartmouth Park) and Carters Green.

Designed by Edward Pincher and built by Mr. J. Dallow, the Farley Memorial Clock Tower still stands today at the Carters Green end of the High Street. It was built in 1897 and is an imposing red brick gothic structure 67 feet high with rich terracotta facings. The lower stage of the tower features three relief panels in moulded frames by Albert Hopkins (who later became master of the Ryland Art School). The panels depict West Bromwich Town Hall, the Oak House and a profile head and shoulders portrait of Farley himself. The clock has a face on each of the four sides and the tower is surmounted by a segmented domed roof with weather vane.

THE APPEAL LETTER

Mayor's Parlour
Town Hall, West Bromwich
May 1896
Dear Sir,
As you are probably aware the Town Committee lately conferred the Honorary Freedom of the Borough upon Alderman Farley and at a representative meeting it was thought that this would be a suitable time to give the friends of Alderman Farley an opportunity to show their appreciation of his public services.

It is now upwards of 30 years since Alderman Farley entered upon public work. During that time he has been a member of the Board of Commissioners of which he was Chairman 9 times, a member of the Council 13 years being five times elected Mayor. He has also served on the Board of Guardians, School Board, Institute Council and Hospital Board. There has been perhaps no movement of importance either public, social or charitable in which he has not taken interest.

He has crowned various acts showing his lively interest in the Borough by presenting a Public Park at Greets Green and the old Oak House as gifts to the town. It has therefore been decided (after having obtained the approval of Alderman Farley) to erect a Clock Tower at the junctions of roads at Carters Green, West Bromwich which will, in a slight degree, commemorate the public works of Alderman Farley.

I appeal with confidence to you to join in this movement and should you feel inclined to subscribe, shall be glad if you will fill in the enclosed form and return the same either to me or any of the Banks in West Bromwich.

Yours faithfully,
Geo. Salter
Mayor

The estimated cost of the Tower and Clock, together with Architect's Commission, sundries, etc. is £800.

THE FARLEY CLOCK TOWER – OPENING CEREMONY

The article published in *The Free Press* of Friday October 29, 1897 revealed just how important Reuben Farley had been to West Bromwich during the 48 years he had been engaged in the public work of the town. The subscribers who contributed to the cost of erecting the Clock Tower included the members of all the public authorities, private individuals, working men and in fact every section of the community.

On Wednesday October 27 the proceedings began with a luncheon at the Masonic Hall attended by those intimately connected with Alderman Farley in either a public or private capacity. Councillor George Salter, who was the Chairman of the Committee responsible for the movement to erect the clock tower, presided over the event.

Following the various addresses Reuben responded:

> *"In early life they were prone, he thought, to look forward to the life of the future, but as they grew older they were perhaps more prone to become retrospective than prospective. He should perhaps be excused therefore if that afternoon he asked them to look backward over the last 25 or 30 years.*
>
> *Those present who remembered West Bromwich of 25 or 30 years ago would know that it was very different then from what it was today. He had occasionally met West Bromwich men who had returned after a long absence in the Colonies or the United States and they expressed themselves as very much astonished at the changes for the better which had taken place in West Bromwich during their absence.*
>
> *Looking back to the time of the old Commissioners, before the town obtained a charter of incorporation, they found the Free Libraries Act was sensibly and wisely adopted and the Public Buildings were erected including the Town Hall, Free Library, Market Hall and Baths. Dartmouth Park was laid out, the Gas Undertaking acquired, Friar Park purchased and a system of deep drainage was begun. There were medical men present and they could tell them better than he could that it was impossible to exaggerate the importance of sanitation. A very distinguished authority had said that health is the first wealth.*
>
> *The Corporation, with its higher civic life, had nobly carried on the work begun by the old Commissioners and the remarkable progress and improvements which had been made since the incorporation needed no comment from him. At their Mayoral banquets was it not written in the book of chronicles that the Mayor for the time being delighted and properly so, to give some record of the progress made during his year of office. He did not propose to take up much time that afternoon with*

regard to those past years because it was something like a thrice-told tale. They had had it repeated so many times in the Town Hall that there was no occasion for him to travel over it again.

Even during this Jubilee year two public parks had been opened in West Bromwich, one in Spon Lane and the other in Hill Top Ward and it was impossible to exaggerate the importance of these places for they formed something like the lungs of a town and tended to raise the moral tone and to increase the health and longevity of the people. One other thing he desired to mention was the building of additional class rooms at the Institute for applied art to manufacturing industries. Everyone would appreciate this as a step in the right direction. The Corporation did a wise thing by adopting the Technical Instruction Act and taking over the schools at the Institute. The schools were doing a great work and the members of the Town Council, and he thought West Bromwich men generally, were proud of them. The Art school especially stood in the foremost rank of art schools in the United Kingdom. It would ever be a source of unalloyed pleasure to him that he had been permitted to take some humble part in all this progressive work during the last 25 or 30 years.

It had been his good fortune when in office to be supported by loyal colleagues and he should ever retain a grateful recollection of this loyal support and especially at the time when they had that big fight with Birmingham. He would not detain them further except to again express his gratitude for the honour conferred upon him."

The lunch was followed by a ceremony at Carters Green led by Councillor Salter.

The tower had been designed by a West Bromwich architect. The medallion of Alderman Farley and the representations of the public buildings and the Oak House were the work of a student and master in the Art Classes. The terracotta panels were supplied and burnt by Mr. Joseph Hamblett. He thought Alderman Farley would be one of the first to appreciate the fact that it was West Bromwich workmanship.

The Mayor, Councillor Akrill accepted the tower on behalf of the town. He thought it very fitting that some memorial should have been erected of Alderman Farley's splendid services and generosity to the town. He was glad Alderman Farley could be present and hoped that his children were somewhere about that day witnessing the testimony to their father's worth and that would be an incentive to them to follow his noble footsteps.

He told the gathering that Mr. Farley reminded him of a visit he made to Ross on Wye. He had only been there a short time before he heard of a man the town still delighted to honour for his generous actions over 173 years before. The man was not known by his own name but as the man of Ross. As time went on he felt

Alderman Farley would come to be looked upon in the same way. He would be known not so much as Alderman Farley as 'The Man of West Bromwich'.

Another tale he told that day referred to a watchmaker's epitaph he had read in a Welsh churchyard:

"Here lies in a horizontal position, the outward case of George Rutleigh, watchmaker, whose abilities in that line were an honour to his profession. Integrity was the main spring and prudence the regulator of all the actions of his life. Human, honest and industrious, his hands never stopped until he had relieved distresses. He had the art of disposing of his time in such a way that he never went wrong except when set going by persons who did not know his key and even then was easily set right again".

The Mayor said the epitaph would apply to Reuben Farley although he recalled hearing the Alderman say that when he passed away he would desire no other epitaph written concerning him than that during a long life, he did all that in him lay, to raise and improve the condition of his native town. These were noble words.

Alderman Farley, who spoke with deep feeling, remarked that he was too full to say much on the occasion. He, however, appreciated very highly the honour which had been conferred upon him by the erection of this memorial. He felt grateful to the Mayor and Councillor Salter for the eulogiums they had passed upon him and wished he could feel that he more thoroughly deserved them. He was, however grateful for what had been done to show appreciation of his humble services. In what he had done he had never done anything for the sake of popularity. It had never been a question with him whether a thing was popular or not popular but had certainly been a question of whether it was right and a good thing for the town and people of West Bromwich. He hoped the tower would serve the purpose of an incentive to the young men of today to do all they could in their day and generation to help forward the good old town of West Bromwich in the safe path of progress and improvement. He felt grateful to their friend Councillor Salter, who was the son of one of the dearest friends he ever had and was glad he had been chairman of this committee. The matter had been in good hands and they had done more than he deserved. He would now close by again returning the most sincere and heartfelt thanks for the honour they had conferred upon him.

It was not so long ago that the stretch of West Bromwich High Street from the milestone at The Fox & Dogs public house to the milestone on Carters Green was known as 'The Golden Mile'. How fitting then that there is a reminder of Reuben Farley at each end – the Farley Fountain at Dartmouth Square and the Farley Clock Tower at Carters Green.

CHAPTER NINE

A Sudden Ending

REPORTS ON THE DEATH OF REUBEN FARLEY

The Free Press Friday March 17, 1899

Alderman Farley, who has been a foremost figure in the public life of the town for many years, whose name was known, loved and honoured far beyond the confines of our town, is no more. The end came with almost appalling suddenness. Although it was known he was not well comparatively few people were aware of the dangerous character of his illness.

It is hardly necessary to say that the unhappy event has plunged the whole town into deepest mourning. By his genial bearing, his faithful public work, abounding generosity and high moral character, Mr. Farley had endeared himself not only to those associated with him by family ties, or in public work, but to the whole population of the Borough. For close upon fifty years he laboured zealously and untiringly to promote the interest of his native town and placed at its disposal abilities of no mean order. During a very large part of this time he was looked upon as the leader in all that pertained to the local government of the town and to every institution with which it was associated – and they were many – his name gave weight, influence and dignity. He knew how to accept both victory and defeat, could both give and receive hard knocks in argument, but whether it was on the winning or the losing side he fought, he did so with good temper and singular freedom from personal feeling. He was quick to forget a wrong ready with counsel and advice and those who enjoyed the privilege of his personal friendship will specially reverence his memory. During his long busy and useful career he was connected at one time or another with all our public institutions and the town is full of memorials of his faithful labours, his influence and his munificence. The fact that West Bromwich possesses the right to manufacture and supply its own gas is due to his initiative, public spirit and untiring work and everybody knows with what rare devotion he has served us as Chairman of the Gas Committee. We owe it to his forethought, and his friendship and influence with the late Lord Dartmouth that we have such a magnificent breathing place as Dartmouth Park and he not only encouraged the movement but set a splendid example in the provision of parks for the outlaying parts of the Borough. One other portion of his work in which he took a special delight was that he did in association with the late Mr. Ryland and other large-hearted gentlemen, some of them still happily with us, in connection with the West Bromwich Institute. He took an active part in the movement which led to the erection of the handsome building in Lodge Road, helped it liberally from his purse and by his unceasing personal effort and interest as a member of the Committee.

We all recognise that by Alderman Farley's death the town has experienced an irreparable loss, but it is as impossible to adequately and accurately realise and measure up that loss at present as it is to properly assess the value of a life such as his, so full of activity, of unceasing effort for the good of others and of great and noble-minded generosity. When he began his public work West Bromwich was a small and comparatively unimportant place. Today it is an important and prosperous town, ahead of many of its neighbours and with a population of over 60000. How much of its progress and importance do we not owe to the working of the brain now stilled by death and to the progressive influence Alderman Farley exerted! He has certainly left West Bromwich far better than he found it and has secured in an unstinted measure that reward he always assured us was, next to the satisfying of his own conscience, the only ambition he had in his public work – the goodwill and affection of his fellow townsmen.

To Mrs. Farley and the sorrowing family the hearts of the people of West Bromwich will go out in deep, strong sympathy. Our hope is that they may be providentially strengthened in the trial they are called upon to bear and that the remembrance of the activity, the nobility and the sweetness of the life that has closed, and the bright influence for good that it is certain to have, will be some solace to them in their hour of great sorrow.

— oOo —

The end came about 8.45 on Saturday night when the deceased passed away at his residence, Summerfield Court, Bratt Street, West Bromwich at the age of 73. Toward the close the deceased had intervals of consciousness in which he was able to recognise those about him. He had not been well for some time but hardly anyone expected his illness to have so suddenly fatal a result. A month or so ago he went to Bath in the hope that the waters there would have a beneficial effect and relieve him of the gout from which he was then suffering. Unfortunately the desired improvement did not take place and he returned to West Bromwich really no better.

He continued however to attend to his public duties till the early part of last week, when he was compelled to remaining indoors and his condition became such as to cause great anxiety to his friends. On the Thursday morning there was a distinct improvement, but in the afternoon there was again a change. The malady from which he was suffering affected the heart and his medical attendant and close personal friend, Mr. Alderman Underhill, who was almost constantly in the sick room, at once sent for Dr. Simon. The latter saw the patient the same evening, again on the Friday and a third time on the Saturday morning. At the latter period, we are informed, partial paralysis had set in and the care was regarded as practically hopeless. The patient had become unconscious but had lost all pain. He gradually sank and died, as stated, at 8.45. When the news of the end got abroad the municipal flag was promptly hoisted half-mast at the Town Hall. Flags were similarly hoisted at both entrances to Dartmouth Park and at the Fire Station and there were many evidences of the deep sorrow of the town and their sympathy with the bereaved family. The certified cause of death, it may be mentioned, was angina pectoris.

— oOo —

PULPIT REFERENCES
The Free Press Friday March 17, 1899

Following the sudden death of Reuben Farley the local press reported that many of the West Bromwich churches made reference to him during their Sunday services.

Christ Church

Reuben was a regular worshiper at Christ Church. A former vicar of the church, Archdeacon Hodgson, spoke of the great loss sustained by the town in the loss of a man who had always shown a keen interest in its social and commercial development. At the evening service the vicar Rev. C.W. Carrington reminded the congregation that it was only last Sunday that Alderman Farley had received the Holy Communion at that altar and it was probably the last act in which he had publicly joined with old friends. They could only look back on his blameless life where thought, word and deed rang true to each other like a bell without a flaw.

St. John's Church

At the evening service the Vicar Ref. N.T. Langley referred to Reuben as an old and intimate personal friend and testified to the excellent public service he had rendered the Borough for many years.

Golds Green Chapel

At Golds Green Chapel where the Mayor conducted the service, he said that God gave to everyone a work to do in life and when that work was done the summons came to depart. The deceased Alderman began early in life to improve himself intellectually and formed a good and noble character which stood him in good stead all his life. He had mapped out for him by Providence a life's work which included the improvement and elevation of his native town.

Wesley Chapel

Preaching at Wesley Chapel the Rev. Enoch Salt made sympathetic reference to the death of Alderman Farley. He understood that Reuben had been connected with the church in his youth and though he had since become a member of another communion his sympathy had not been withdrawn from them. It was not as members of a church they mourned the loss of Mr. Farley but as members of a community of citizens for whose corporate welfare he had laboured so devotedly. He hoped the youth of the town would follow in his footsteps and give themselves as he had done, for the service of their fellows.

Lyng

Rev. W.C. Rose preaching at the Lyng commented on the flags flying at half-mast on the public buildings proclaiming a public loss and symbolising a respect, a love, an admiration for his character and life. He was one who took an intense and intelligent interest in all that belonged to the advancement of the town and its life.

THE FUNERAL Wednesday 15, March, 1899

The Free Press

Reuben's funeral was reported in the local press to be "one of a very imposing and impressive character", words often used to describe the man himself.

Complying with a request by the Mayor many of the shops in the town closed at noon. Some manufacturers gave a holiday to their employees and most private houses and business premises drew their blinds giving the town a very mournful appearance.

Mrs. Farley had expressed her desire that the proceedings should be as quiet as possible and only a very few people therefore met at the house. However the feeling in the town was so intense that it was impossible to prevent a demonstration of sorrow and sympathy. The hearse containing the body of the deceased left Summerfield Court shortly before three o'clock and was immediately followed by two carriages containing floral tributes. Behind those came the mourners and private friends.

Amongst the mourners were Masters Reuben and Charles Farley, sons of the deceased, Mr. R. Fellows, Mr. Alderman Underhill (deceased's medical attendant), Mr. J.H. Pearson, Alderman Rollason, Mr. Joshua Fellows, Mr. E. Caddick (deceased's solicitor), Mr. G.H. Claughton and the Rev. N.T. Langley (executors).

The bearers were Messrs. A. Camwell, E. Aston, T. Pearce, W. Spooner, E. Vaughan, T. Jones, W. Stambridge, T. Otway, S. Mills and D. Cole, employees at the Summit Foundry.

Those who were to take part in the public procession having assembled at the Town Hall walked over to Christ Church where the service was being held.

The official order of the procession was reported as follows:

Fire Brigade
Hearse
Mourning Coaches
the late Alderman's carriage,
The Town Council

> Borough Officials
> County and Borough Magistrates,
> Messrs Taylor and Farley's workpeople
> Institute Council and Officials
> Guardians and Officials
> School Board and Officials
> Hospital Board of Management
> West Bromwich Building Society
> Foresters
> Friendly Societies Clubs etc. etc.

The arrangements for the procession were in the hands of the Town Clerk (Mr. A. Caddick) and Chief Superintendent Whitehurst.

The Borough Member Mr. Ernest Spencer walked among the County and Borough Justices. With the Mayor (Councillor Pitt), and Deputy Mayor (Councillor Akrill), was the Town Clerk (Mr. A. Caddick). Alderman J.H. Blades and Councillors S. Baggott, G. Salter, S. Keys, W.H. Keys, G. Darby, J.H. Chesshire, J. Peters, H. Hartland, J.E. Wilson, A.G. Turley, H.L. Browne and S. Withers.

Of the great number of people attending were representatives of Taylor & Farley, Fellows Morton and Clayton, the Glaenavon Steel Company of South Wales, the South Staffordshire Ironfounders Association, the Tradesmens Association, the West Bromwich Charity Football Association, the "Reuben Farley" Lodge of Oddfellows.

Following the service in Christ Church the long funeral cortège, including 60 private carriages, proceeded on its way to the cemetery. In the area around the church and Town Hall a great but orderly and sympathetic crowd had assembled. Chief Superintendent Whitehurst had a large force of police there to keep the way clear for the procession but very little trouble was experienced. The route taken to the cemetery was via Sandwell Road and Hargate Lane and throughout the journey the same sympathetic interest was shown.

At the cemetery too there was a large orderly crowd. The remains were interred in a newly constructed vault which Mr. Farley had only recently selected. Archdeacon Hodgson and the Rev. C.W. Carrington conducted the graveside service.

The coffin was of polished oak with brass mountings and was covered with the lovely wreaths including those from Mr. Fellows and family, Lord and Lady Dartmouth and the Mayor and Mayoress of West Bromwich.

LETTER FROM MRS. FARLEY
to the Free Press,
March 1899

Sir,
Will you allow me to express, through your paper, my gratitude to the public officials of the town, the many private friends in the district and to all the inhabitants of West Bromwich for their most kind expression of sympathy with me and respect to my dear husband. I have been greatly touched by it and am quite unable to say to everyone how much I have felt it, except through the medium of the press.

Yours faithfully,
H.E. Farley,
Summerfield Court, West Bromwich.

OBITUARY
Frederick B. Ludlow

ALDERMAN REUBEN FARLEY, J.P., Summerfield Court, Bratt Street, West Bromwich; youngest son of the late Thomas Farley, who was a mining engineer; born at Newtown, West Bromwich on January 27, 1826 and educated at Borwick Heath House Academy; died on March 11, 1899.

On leaving school Mr. Farley was apprenticed to the late Alderman Cooksey as a mining surveyor, but on the expiration of his apprenticeship acquired and developed the Dunkirk Colliery, his commercial interests increasing with years, until at the time of his death he was head of the firm of Taylor and Farley; Chairman of Directors of the Hamstead Colliery Company; Chairman of the Directors of Danks and Co., Oldbury; Chairman of Fellows, Morton and Clayton and Chairman of the South Staffordshire Ironfounders' Association. At the age of eighteen he began to take an interest in the West Bromwich Institute for the Advancement of Knowledge, afterwards becoming Assistant Secretary, and this gave him his first taste for public work. We are merely stating bare fact when we say that for fifty years Mr. Farley was closely identified with the local governing bodies and with practically all the philanthropic and educational movements of the district. He was a member of the old Board of Improvement Commissioners from 1852 to 1884, being appointed Chairman in 1874, and during his tenure of office the public buildings were completed, and the right acquired to manufacture and supply gas, Mr. Farley being soon afterwards made Chairman of the Gas

Committee, an office held until his death. When the Charter was secured, he was, in 1882, elected as first Mayor of the Borough, being re-elected the following year, and again invited, but declined, thinking the honour should be shared by his colleagues. He again held office in the Jubilee year of 1887, and yet again in 1893-94 and in 1894-95. He was an active member of the first School Board and an ardent supporter of the municipalisation of the Science and Art Schools, and had the satisfaction of seeing this scheme brought to a successful issue. Between 1852 and 1867 he was a member of the West Bromwich Board of Guardians, and was a Trustee of the Almshouses, himself finding a supply of coal for the winter and a gift of money at Christmas for each of the inmates. He was an early supporter of the volunteer movement, having been enrolled in the local company when it was established in 1859. Alderman Farley was repeatedly the recipient of various marks of esteem from his fellow-townsmen. In 1885 he was presented by the Town Council with a life-size portrait in oils, and during his mayoralty, in 1894, on the occasion of the birth of his fourth child, with a silver cradle. On April 20, 1896, in recognition of continued services, and his munificent gift to the town of Oak House and grounds, he had the honour of being made the first Freeman of West Bromwich, and even then a further movement resulted in the erection of the Farley Memorial Clock Tower at Carters Green. Alderman Farley remained single until he reached the age of forty, and has since been married three times, his third wife, who survives him, being a sister of Mr. Joshua Fellows. Of the first two marriages there was no issue, but of the last there are five children, all of whom are living, and one of whom bears his father's name. A Churchman in religion, he yet gave generously to Nonconformist Institutions. In politics he was a Liberal Unionist, but did not take a prominent part.

Alderman Farley has left behind him an ineradicable record of public work well and faithfully done.

WILL OF REUBEN FARLEY

The will of the late Alderman R. Farley, of West Bromwich, dated August 13 1896, was proved on 26 May, 1899, by the surviving Executors, Mr. Gilbert H. Claughton and the Rev. Norton Theodore Langley. The gross value of the estate was sworn at £167,734 16s.9d.

Reuben's last will was drawn up just after the birth of his youngest child and the main beneficiaries of his real estate were his sons, (left in Trust until they reached the age of 21 years).

To his eldest son Reuben Llewellyn:
The Highfield estate comprising of dwelling houses in High Street and Sandwell Road. Also Reuben's residence at the time he died.

To second son Charles Finch:
The Springfield and Oakley estates.

To youngest son Francis Dashwood:
The estate at Newbury Lane, Oldbury, the Dunkirk estate West Bromwich, and several properties in and near Cutlers End and Dartmouth Street, West Bromwich.

To his wife Harriet he left his household effects and an annuity of £2000 per year during her widowhood.

All his residuary estate was devised to his trustees in trust for sale, to be held in trust for his sons and daughters in equal share.

The Silver Cradle was left to daughter Clara Helena, the child born during the year of his mayoralty in 1894. All the illuminated addresses and other gifts presented to him by public bodies or workmen were left to son Reuben Llewellyn.

There were several bequests to his works managers and clerks. His domestic servants were not forgotten providing they had been in his service for the two years before his death. Some servants were singled out for special bequests such as his coachman William Adbury and his cook Elizabeth Bloomer. Even his mother's old servant Charlotte Smith was remembered.

A sum of £3200 was left to be shared between the surviving brothers and sisters of his late wife, Elizabeth Farley.

From reports in the *West Bromwich Chronicle* on April 28 and May 26 1899 it would appear that there was much speculation in the town regarding the possible value of Reuben's estate with figures of £100,000 and £250,000 mentioned. Perhaps because he had been such a generous donor to so many local projects during his lifetime there might be a further bequest in his will? However, apart from £1,000 left to the Endowment Fund of West Bromwich Hospital no public institutions would benefit.

HEATH LANE CEMETERY

The West Bromwich Improvement Commissioners purchased 16 acres of land in 1858 at a cost of £6400. Birmingham Architect Edward Holmes designed the Lodge and two chapels of which only the lodge remains today.

Reuben was buried here on Wednesday March 15, 1899. It would seem that at the time of his death he had only recently selected the plot where his vault would be built. When his wife Harriet died in August 1938 she too was buried there.

A number of Reuben's friends and peers were buried close by. In life they sat side by side on various boards and committees and in death would remain close together for all time. The Salter family plot is immediately next to Farley's and just behind are those of William Burch, another West Bromwich Improvement Commissioner and Henry Browne who was for 30 years Superintendent of Dartmouth Park.

Even antagonist George Wilkes is buried close by on the opposite side of the path. Curiously it was reported that in 1864, ten years before his death, 'Barber' Wilkes visited the cemetery with a group of his friends including Mr. Brough, who laid the memorial brick of the tomb where George would be buried.

Some family members are close by too. Reuben's sister Susannah and her husband George Taylor had been buried a few rows behind some years earlier.

Over the years the inscriptions on Reuben and Harriet's gravestone had faded but the restoration funded by their great grandson Tom Farley was completed in June 2014. On Saturday June 14th a rededication service was performed at the graveside by Rev. Andrew Smith of All Saints Church. Tom and his family attended together with members of the West Bromwich Local History Society and Mayor Derek Rowley who wore the Mayoral Chain first worn by Reuben.

CHAPTER TEN

The Farley Residences

BIRTHPLACE OF REUBEN FARLEY
From Old West Bromwich 83 13.10.44

146 Whitehall Road has the distinction of being the birthplace of Reuben Farley. His father was Thomas Farley, a mining engineer. It was a modest house, double-fronted, with ordinary flat windows and three steps up to the front door.

Born on January 27, 1826* Reuben was the youngest son and the eighth of ten children. His father died when he was less than 9 years old so he lived with his mother for many years during which time he attained wealth and distinction. It was at the age of 40 that he left to get married. Elizabeth Farley could have left the neighbourhood to occupy a house more in keeping with her son's social position but she stayed in the old home until her death on February 24, 1885. Her son acknowledged the immense debt he owed to her for all she had done for him throughout his early life and erected a drinking fountain in Dartmouth Square to commemorate her memory.

Reuben too had an abiding affection for the place of his birth and one expression of it was the gift of Farley Park.

It is difficult for us today to conjure up a mental picture of what Great Bridge and Greets Green was like when Reuben Farley was a boy. The large mansions have long since gone but he would have known White Hall on the site which is now Farley Park and Cop Hall which was in the angle formed by the junction of Whitehall Road and Sheepwash Lane. The fields and woodlands had slowly disappeared as mining and industry took over.

Between White Hall and Cop Hall there was a little group of houses forming three small streets named respectively: Finch, Frances and Rogers Street. They were known as Paul's New Town and apparently derived that name from Sir Horace St. Paul Bart of Ewoods Park, Northumberland. He was a large landowner in Tipton and also the possessor of the land between Dunkirk and Great Bridge known as the Pump House Estate. In 1849 his West Bromwich holding extended to 56 acres and included the Pump House Colliery. Finch Street probably derived its name from the F. Finch who in 1837 owned considerable land in the Great Bridge district though by 1849 his name disappeared from the list of landowners. The church of St. Peter was erected in 1858 and the ecclesiastical parish formed three years later.

*Although most references to Reuben's date of birth show it as January 27, 1826 the Farley family bible entry records the event as January 27, 1825 at 12 o'clock at night.

Reuben Farley, Son of Thomas and Elizabeth Farley was born at Great Bridge, January 27th, 1825, at 12 o'clock at night.

The Farley Residences
Information taken from the U.K. Census Returns 1841 to 1911

1841
Foundry Yard
Cambridge
Edwin Farley 25
Honour Farley 25
Sarah Farley 3
Elizabeth Farley 1
Reuben Farley 15

Reuben is staying with
his brother in Cambridge

1851
Oldbury Lane
West Bromwich
Elizabeth Farley 58
John Farley 36
Reuben Farley gson 5
Betsey Farley 21
Reuben Farley 24

John is a widower

1861
Oldbury Rd to Farley St
West Bromwich
Elizabeth Farley 68

Reuben Farley 36
Charlotte Smith (servant)

1871
Whitehall Road
Elizabeth Farley 78
Charlotte Smith (servant)

1881
146 Whitehall Road
Elizabeth Farley 88
Charlotte Smith (servant)
Mary Hughes (servant)

1891

New Street
Reuben Farley 45
Hannah Farley 42
Ellen Beard (servant)
Wm. Barnes (groom/gardener)

14 New Street
Reuben Farley 55
Elizabeth Farley 39
Mary Hodgkiss (servant)
Elizabeth Jones (servant)

14 New Street
Reuben Farley 65
Harriet E Farley 36
Edith M Farley 2
Reuben L Farley 9 mo
Elizabeth Bloomer (cook)
Elizabeth Jones (housemaid)
Agnes Clemon (nursery maid)

1901
Bratt Street
Harrietta Farley 46
E Margaret Farley 12 dau
Reuben L Farley 10 son
Charles F Farley 8 son
Clara H Farley 6 dau
Francis D Farley 4 son
Elizabeth Bloomer (housekeeper)
Emma J Parkes (parlour maid)
Alice G Hayward (nursemaid)
Lizzie James (housemaid)

1911 Sunday April 2nd
Summerfield Court/Bratt Street
Harrietta E Farley 56
Margaret Farley 22
Reuben Farley 20

Francis Farley 14

Alice Hayward (housemaid)
Lilly Bradley (parlourmaid)

14 NEW STREET, "Cambridge House"

Reuben married three times from 1867 to 1887 and each wife lived at his New Street residence. In 1887, the year of his marriage to Harriette Emily Fellows, he extended the property with the plans being approved on March 29. Further additions were planned in March 1890 which included a new bedroom and nursery to accommodate their growing family.

Cambridge House (No. 14 New Street) no longer stands but the 1911 census listed Dicken Athletic Outfitters at number 12, a property which survives today. In subsequent years the Palais De Dance (later the Adelphi) stood next door until it was destroyed by fire in 1971. Over the years a number of Reuben's close neighbours were medical men. At No. 16 was Dr. Sansome in 1861 and R. Trimble (surgeon) in 1891. Dr. John Manley lived at No. 20 (1871/1881/1891 census). Another close neighbour in 1871 was Samuel Keys. Also located in New Street was the office of Edward Caddick, solicitor. His brother Alfred, also a solicitor, went on to become the first Town Clerk of the Borough. All important men in the town at that time.

After Reuben and his family moved from No. 14 New Street it was occupied by surgeon Arthur Stopford Underhill (1901 census), son of Alderman Underhill.

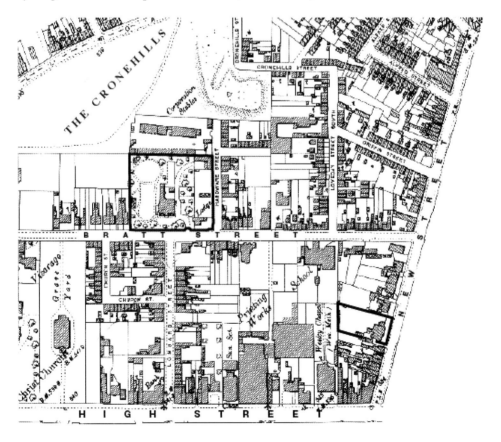

By 1911 the occupant was Viscount Lewisham who succeeded as the seventh Earl of Dartmouth. From 1910 to 1918 he was the M.P. for West Bromwich.

SUMMERFIELD HOUSE

By the mid 1890s Reuben could easily have retired and moved out of the town, away from the noise and smoking chimneys of industry but he chose not to. Instead he decided to buy a large property in Bratt Street and spent a great deal of money improving it. The plans drawn up by Wood and Kendrick were approved on November 9, 1897 and showed the extent of Reuben's additions and alterations to 'Summerfield'. A stable block and lodge were also added.

On the 1911 census Harriet recorded that there were 14 rooms at Summerfield Court.

Reuben and Harriet held many fundraising events at Summerfield which were reported in the local newspapers of the day and after Reuben's death Harriet continued with her involvement. In March 1902 she was President of the West Bromwich Division of the Soldier's & Sailor's Association.

Another Mayor (1884-5) occupied Summerfield before Reuben. It was the family home of a close personal friend, Alderman Thomas Underhill.

The house no longer stands although the lodge still remains. Until 2013 the building was still recognisable as the lodge but has since been completely renovated into a two-story property.

AFTER WEST BROMWICH

SANDY LODGE, BEDFORDSHIRE

After Reuben's death Harriet lived at Summerfield Court with her young family for some years until she moved to Sandy Lodge, Bedford, the property built by a son of former Prime Minister Sir Robert Peel in 1870. 'Mrs. Farley' was listed as occupier of Sandy Lodge in the 1914 and 1920 County Directory. Daughter Clara Helena married in Sandy, Bedfordshire in 1920.

Today the Grade II listed building is the headquarters of the R.S.P.B.

WORNDITCH HALL, KIMBOLTON, HUNTINGDONSHIRE

It was about 1920 when Reuben Llewellyn Farley bought Wornditch Hall, set in 64 acres of garden, parkland and woodland with the River Kym running through it. The property was Grade II listed April 28, 1983 and described as eighteenth century of local brick.

When his mother Harriette died on August 31, 1938 her address was given as Wornditch Hall.

HARBURY, LEAMINGTON SPA, WARWICKSHIRE

Three of the Farley children settled in Harbury, living quite close to each other.

Edith Margaret lived at 41 Farm Street.

Charles Finch Farley died at Manor Stable, Harbury in 1969 but prior to that his residence was Wisset Lodge in Church Street. When it became a Grade II listed building on May 30, 1967 it was described as a mid/late seventeenth century house with earlier origins.

The Manor House, Park Lane was the residence of Francis Dashwood Farley. It was a substantial house positioned in the heart of the village. This too became a Grade II listed building on May 30, 1967 when it was described as mid sixteenth century with seventeenth and eighteenth century additions and alterations. Timber framed with brick infill. Further additions and alterations were made in the twentieth century. Several rooms had oak panelling.

FARLEY FAMILY CONTACT TODAY

Research on another project led to Anne making contact firstly with Jonathan and then Tom Farley. Both men were interested in our research into their important ancestor and have visited West Bromwich several times over the past few years. Jonathan has kindly allowed us to include his Farley family history research and Tom has provided us with many family images.

Tom has visited West Bromwich on several occasions in support of the Friends of Dartmouth Park. The first visit in June 2011 was to attend an exhibition at the Town Hall which documented Reuben's life and achievements, some of the items on display being supplied by Tom himself.

Reuben's mayoral robe and chain of office were also on display. An opportunity then for Tom to try on the chain presented to his great grandfather by Lord Dartmouth.

Extra links have been added over the years.

Tom also visited Reuben and Harriet's grave in Heath Lane Cemetery.

Continuing contact with Tom has resulted in him funding the complete restoration of the Farley gravestone and with his kind permission, West Bromwich Local History Society have added a granite tablet showing Reuben's importance as the first and five times Mayor of West Bromwich.

CHAPTER ELEVEN

History Of The Farley Family

HISTORY OF THE FARLEY FAMILY NAMES

Robin Pearson

Reuben Farley's great grandfather chose a significant but costly year to be married. A new law, aimed at ending clandestine marriages, imposed different rules with regard to the publication of banns at the church where the ceremony would be performed. Licences were required to marry under any variation of the conditions and a surety had to be paid to the bishop's diocese in which the couple normally lived.

A collier, Thomas Farly, whose name was spelt without an 'e', was married to Elizabeth Jervis on 4 March 1753. He had previously paid a bond of £100, a considerable sum for the time, to the Dean of Lichfield Cathedral. When the couple died respectively in 1792 he was buried as Fairly and in 1798 she was recorded as Fairley. Their four children were all baptised with the surname Fearley and the third boy when he died, age 61, was named as Edward Farley. Today the name is clearly visible on his slate gravestone in the churchyard at Great Brington. This Northamptonshire church of St. Mary houses the tombs of the ancestors of George Washington, Princess Diana, and West Bromwich's first Catholic priest of the nineteenth century.

Buried near to Edward, mentioned above, at Great Brington is his niece Ann, the second child of his eldest brother, John, the grandfather of Reuben the future Mayor. Ann's husband was a farmer called Reuben Main. Apart from the Mayor's first son being called Reuben there would be two nephews and a great nephew bearing that name.

Another name running in the family is Dashwood, the maiden name of Reuben Farley's grandmother. His fifth child would have Dashwood as one of his names as in the case of Reuben's grandson and great grandson.

A third family name is Llewelyn which was given to the first child of Mayor Reuben and his third wife Harriette – Reuben Llewelyn Farley the future High Sheriff of Cambridgeshire and Huntingdonshire. The Welsh name belonged to the Mayor's mother, Elizabeth, whose memory is perpetuated in West Bromwich's High Street Farley Fountain. At the time of Elizabeth's wedding to Thomas Farly her surname was Llewellin with their marriage register entry adding an extra 'g'. In the Farley Family Bible Elizabeth's surname is spelt as a third variant in the form of Lleawelyn. A further variant found in the name of the Mayor's brother, John's second boy as Levi Lewellyn Farley.

Much of the above information is based on the family research undertaken by Jonathan Farley, the great, great grandson of John Farley, one of the Mayor's brothers.

On the following pages Jonathan recounts the details of the lives of Reuben Farley's siblings and some of their descendants.

THE FARLEY FAMILY

Jonathan Farley

REUBEN FARLEY'S SIBLINGS AND SOME OF THEIR DESCENDENTS

Susannah Farley
Born 5th November 1810, Bilston, baptised 1st January 1811, Bilston. Married George Taylor by banns at Bushbury on 5th August 1833. Her brother Reuben was head of the Summit Foundry, bought with brother-in-law George in 1861. It became the largest of its kind in South Staffordshire.

Thomas Farley
Born 3rd September 1812, Bilston, baptised 11th October 1812, Bilston. Died 13th April 1843 of consumption. His occupation was a mine agent, and Ann (née Peacock), wife of brother Fredrick, was present at his death.

John Farley, my great, great grandfather.
Born 4th May 1814, Bilston, baptised 4th May 1814, Bilston. He may have been premature, hence his baptism on the same day. Married Sarah Stanton at St Martins, Birmingham, 18th June 1837. Sarah was the daughter of John and Ellen Stanton, and baptised at All Saints on 16th March 1812. Her father was a shoemaker of Virgins End, West Bromwich. John, an engineer, and Sarah lived at Great Bridge, West Bromwich. They had three children – Thomas, Levi Lewellyn and Reuben.

Sarah died on 13th May 1848, aged 31 years, in Smethwick. John was present at the death.

On 14th April 1851 John remarried to Emily Reavenhall at Harborne St Peter.

Her father William Reavenhall was also an engineer, and probably worked with John.

John and Emily had two children: Mary Ann born 18th October 1854 and Louis born 16th March 1856. Both of them at Cranford Street, Smethwick.

On July 27th, 1858, two years after Louis was born, Emily died. Once again in the family, Phthisis, or Consumption of the lungs, had struck. In attendance was Susan Clark, and on the Census of 1861, was looking after the children, Mary Ann and Louis, at their house also in Cranford Street. Meanwhile John was lodging with the Jaques family in Deritend and Reuben and Levi from his first marriage to

Sarah Stanton are staying with their uncle, Lot Shakespeare in West Bromwich. Incidentally, Emily had died at the age of thirty-one, exactly the same age as John's first wife, Sarah.

John died in 1881 at Wednesbury, at the age of sixty-six.

In 1877 their daughter, Mary Ann, had married Joseph Allbrooke, a boat-builder and coal merchant. The family resided at 11 Church Square, Oldbury.

Also in 1877, at the age of twenty-one, my great grandfather Louis married Mary Ann Smith, daughter of Frederick and Lucy, he being a coalmaster. They had six children: William, Emily Ann, Lucy Ellen, Ruth, Reuben Frederick and Joseph Louis.

The family moved to Leicestershire, but on 4th May 1890, Louis died of a heart attack, aged 34.

William, my grandfather, who was born in Maria Street, West Bromwich on 2nd April 1878, decided to join the army.

He enlisted on 8th April 1895, aged 18 and 5'8" tall, a fitter by trade, to the South Staffordshire Regiment, and thence to India where on 30th December 1904 he married Mabel Sullivan at Colaba. By now William had attained the rank of sergeant.

After eighteen years service in the Regiment, William took his pension on 31st May 1913. He became a member of the Birmingham Parks Police unit, and lived in 'The Lodge' Abbey Road, Oldbury at the entrance to Warley Woods. 'The Lodge' was demolished some years ago.

William and Mabel had four children: May, William Joseph, Lucy and Lillian. Lillian was actually born in 'The Lodge.'

In 1915 William rejoined the army as Company Sergeant Major for B Company 15th Royal Warwicks, (2nd Birmingham Battalion.) and received his Commission as Second – Lieutenant on 22nd November 1915.

The Battalion embarked for France and were stationed in the Arras area.

On Thursday 15th June 1916 a whizz bang smashed through the parapet and exploded in the trench held by A. Coy. Four men were killed outright including William Farley.

He is buried in Faubourg D'Amiens Cemetery, Arras. His name is on the memorial at St. Hilda's Church, Oldbury, and also on the Coalville War Memorial, Leicestershire. The book, "Birmingham Pals" by Terry Carter describes the action on that June day in 1916.

His son, William Joseph Farley, was only five when his father died, and as was usual in those days, put in the care of his guardian.

He was educated at St. Lawrence College, Ramsgate, joined the Duke of Cornwall's Light Infantry at the outbreak of the Second World War, and rose to the rank of Major. Later in life he became a Company Director.

William Joseph had lived at the Lodge, Abbey Road, Oldbury during 1913 and 1914.

Frederick Farley

Born 18th May 1816 at Wyken, Warwickshire. On his baptism record at St Laurence Church, 16th June 1816, his father Thomas is entered as a land/mine agent.

The family had moved to Warwickshire for about three years, before moving back to Bilston.

On 20th September 1840, Frederick married Ann Peacock, by licence, in West Bromwich. His profession is a plumber and her father a bailiff.

They had twelve children, and one, Frederick Reuben, drowned after falling into a brook on 6th May 1858, aged two.

At this time Frederick's occupation was an Innkeeper, but it may have been Ann managing the Inn as on 22nd March 1858, Frederick had been sentenced to four years in prison for forgery.

He was tried at Warwick Crown Court for forging a cheque for Three hundred and Forty Pounds (£340), for which the family requested that he "be removed from the country".

The judge replied that as the law stood, he was not empowered to pass a sentence of transportation.

Ann was already pregnant with her tenth child, Helen, who was born in Horseley Heath on 12th November 1858.

Frederick must have been granted some remission as their next child, Frederick William, was born on 2nd June 1862 at Horseley Heath. Their last child, Kate, was born on 1st October 1863, when Frederick's occupation is stated as plumber and glazier.

On Friday 12th July 1872, Frederick was at Warwick Crown Court on a charge of attempted murder on James Hamilton Mark, a bank manager in Upper Priory, Birmingham, for stabbing him in the back. Three people came to the manager's assistance, but were attacked by Frederick with a hammer.

He was sentenced to penal servitude for life.

Due to the scandal, Ann and the children moved to Reading where she became a hotel keeper. On the Census of 1881, Frederick is a prisoner at Princetown, Dartmoor, aged 64. Frederick was moved to Woking Prison in Surrey, where he died on 20th April 1885, aged 68.

Ann (née Peacock) died at St Giles, Reading on 5th September 1888, aged 66.

Edwin Farley

Born 3rd September 1818 at Bilston. On 2nd October 1837, Edwin married Honor Aaron in the parish of Tipton, both of their ages recorded as minors. Her father, Moses Aaron, was an iron founder by profession.

Edwin's occupation is also recorded as an iron founder, but his father's name and profession is left blank. It may be that the family did not approve of the marriage, but brother John, my great, great grandfather, did attend as a witness. In 1838 they moved to Cambridge where they had three children.

On the Census of 1841, brother Reuben, then aged 15, is staying with the family.

Edwin retired when he was sixty and moved by himself to Landport, Portsea Island, where he died on 3rd March 1886, aged 67. The move may have been for his health.

After Edwin's death, Honor moved in with her daughter, Sarah Ann, who had married Herbert Riseley, where she died, in Chesterton, Cambridge on 23rd January 1900 aged 85.

William Farley
Born 24th September 1820, Bilston. Buried St Leonards, Bilston, 28th February 1821, aged 5 months.

Levi Farley
Born 30th November 1822, Bilston. Died 21st September 1842, in West Bromwich, aged 19. Levi died of consumption with brother Frederick present at his death.

Reuben Farley
Born 27th January 1825 at Great Bridge. Died 11th March 1899, aged 73.

Mary Ann Farley
Born 3rd November 1827 at Great Bridge. Died 8th May 1846, aged 18, brother Frederick present at her death.

Betsy Farley
Born 13th January 1830 at Great Bridge. Married Thomas Smith on 28th July 1853 in West Bromwich. Brother Reuben was a witness.

Copies of entries from the Farley Family Bible

Births.

Thomas Farley, the Son of John and Mary Farley was born at Brownhills on the 13th day of February, 1781

Elizabeth Lleawelyn the Daughter of John and Susannah Lleawelyn was born October 18th, 1792 – about 6 o'clock in the morning.

Births.

Susannah Farley, Daughter of Thomas and Elizabeth Farley, was born November 5th 1810 at Bilston 13 minutes past 7 o'clock at night.

Thomas Farley, Son of Thomas and Elizabeth Farley, was born at Bilston September 3rd 1812 at 8 o'clock A.M.

John Farley, Son of Thomas and Elizabeth Farley, was born May 4th 1814, – 10 minutes before 8 o'clock in the morning.

Frederick Farley, Son of Thomas and Elizabeth Farley was born May 18th 1816 – at ½ past 9 o'clock in the morning at Wyken in the County of Warwick.

Edwin Farley, Son of Thomas and Elizabeth Farley, was born at Bilston, September 3rd 1818, at 5 o'clock A.M.

William Farley, Son of Thomas and Elizabeth Farley, was born at Bilston, September 24th 1820, at 5 minutes before 6 o'clock in the morning.

Levi Farley, Son of Thomas and Elizabeth Farley, was born at Bilston November 30th 1822 at 8 o'clock A.M.

Reuben Farley, Son of Thomas and Elizabeth Farley, was born at Great Bridge, January 27th, 1825, at 12 o'clock at night.

Mary Ann Farley, Daughter of Thomas and Elizabeth Farley was born at Great Bridge, November 3rd, 1827, at a quarter past 5 o'clock in the morning,

Betsey Farley, Daughter of Thomas and Elizabeth Farley was born at Great Bridge, January 13th, 1830, at 20 minutes before 2 o'clock in the morning.

_____

Deaths.

William Farley, departed this life, February 23rd, 1821, aged 5 months.

Thomas Farley, departed this life, May 26th, 1830, aged 49 years.

Levi Farley, departed this life September 21st, 1842, aged 20 Years.

Thomas Farley, departed this life, April 13th, 1843, aged 30 years.

Mary Ann Farley, departed this life May 8th, 1846, aged 18 years.